Teach the Way the Brain Learns

Curriculum Themes Build Neuron Networks

Madlon T. Laster

Rowman & Littlefield Education
Lanham • New York • Toronto • Plymouth, UK

KH

Published in the United States of America
by Rowman & Littlefield Education
A Division of Rowman & Littlefield Publishers, Inc.
A wholly owned subsidary of The Rowman & Littlefield Publishing Group, Inc.
4501 Forbes Boulevard, Suite 200, Lanham, Maryland 20706
www.rowmaneducation.com

Estover Road
Plymouth PL6 7PY
United Kingdom

British Library Cataloguing in Publication Information Available

Library of Congress Cataloging-in-Publication Data

Laster, Madlon T., 1935–
  Teach the way the brain learns : curriculum themes build neuron networks / Madlon
T. Laster.
      p. cm.
  Includes bibliographical references.
  ISBN 978-1-60709-136-3 (cloth : alk. paper) — ISBN 978-1-60709-137-0 (pbk. : alk.
paper) — ISBN 978-1-60709-138-7 (electronic)
  1. Learning, Psychology of. 2. Learning—Physiological aspects. 3. Brain. 4.
Education—Curricula. I. Title.
  LB1060.L375 2009
  370.15'23—dc22   2009004077

∞ ™ The paper used in this publication meets the minimum requirements of American
National Standard for Information Sciences—Permanence of Paper for Printed Library
Materials, ANSI/NISO Z39.48-1992.
Manufactured in the United States of America.

12/07/10

This book is dedicated to two dear friends and colleagues, whose ideas, influence, suggestions, and support were indispensable in planning and creating the activities and assignments for the curriculum themes described herein. I will be eternally grateful to Glenne White and Hartley Schearer, colibrarians for Daniel Morgan Middle School from the time the building opened in 1974 until we all retired in the year 2000.

CONTENTS

CONTENTS

LIST OF ILLUSTRATIONS

FOREWORD

This isn't one of those warm-fuzzy-feel-good stories about "a teacher who changed my life." This is a story about a teacher who changed my life.

While I had many good teachers throughout my school years, Madlon Laster was able to do something the others were not—she was able to create a thematic anchor in my life, a center for all of my other learning. This isn't overblown, exaggerated fluff. Her approach to teaching by making connections to multiple subjects in a fundamental way shaped my approach to learning that eventually led to a doctorate, university teaching, and now a growing business creating and consulting for integrated middle-school mathematics curriculum.

How did Madlon do all this in the sixth grade? First, she taught me to read. I don't mean the words or sentences; I already knew that part, but she led me to really care about reading. You see, she got me hooked on the Willard Price series of books—adventures of two brothers named Hal and Roger traveling in wilderness all over the world with their game-collecting father.

She read to us about faraway places like the South Pacific, South America, and Africa. In that year with her, I read a total of seven books by Willard Price, all hardback. I read in the morning before school, at school between breaks, and to the dismay of my parents, under the covers at night with a flashlight. My mom jokes that she would ask if Hal and Roger were coming to dinner.

But it wasn't their stories or just reading that changed my life. Madlon did something else: she linked the adventure themes to the curriculum. She built opportunities in our classroom like asking us to create stories of faraway lands. She and my math/science teacher, George Craig, connected topics where we began the year with a survival unit. An orienteering course started a mathematics unit, where I dug into geometry with gusto because I wanted to use the skills of map and compass during my travels throughout the exotic world.

I eventually came to use all those skills in my *real* life. I learned how to make connections between adventure, math, literacy, and even education and evolutionary sciences. In short, what Madlon did was to give the basic tool of thematic learning and to help me see how to build a bridge to everything around me.

Since the time of her class, I've seen thematic teaching in just about every conceivable manner. For the past eleven years, I've taught a thematically based curriculum, and for six years have worked with a national organization called Expeditionary Learning Schools: Outward Bound, a reform movement impacting one hundred and fifty public schools and forty thousand students across the nation that centers its mission on thematic learning. Student test scores are up. Student learning is way up. Kids love it. And teachers—well, the teachers are on fire, lighting up with joy and happiness about learning! I see fifteen hundred teachers each year at conferences and summits who talk about what *they* are studying that semester!

But I've gotten ahead of myself, because I know and hear teachers each day who say, "I can't do that in my school. It's not a thematically based school." Most schools aren't, and yet, each day I also see teachers crossing that imaginary boundary of their subject in a million ways, teaming with other teachers and making bridges to other curriculum in their own classes.

And really, what other choice is there? The brain is hardwired to learn in a thematic manner. Either we respect that or continue on the ugly path of disjointed learning that afflicts the nation's classrooms and leaves children bored and disengaged, or studying just to receive grades, not for the inherent beauty in learning.

Dr. Laster's book provides a progression to thematic teaching for any teacher in any school or classroom. The author is a tried and true teacher who has forty-two years of experience in a traditional school—thirty years of teaching thematically in a conventional, supposedly subject-discrete school.

Sixty million students will pour into the doors of schools in the United States each day. I urge the five million or so teachers responsible for the sacred space of caring for their education to read this book. I urge you to read this book, not because your students' test scores will go up, even though they will. I urge you to read this book, not because your students will learn more, even though they will. I urge you to read this book because it will lead you to love your profession with passion, and to know you are good at it. You'll have a hundred or a thousand students who will say about you, "That teacher really changed my life."

Scott Laidlaw, Ed.D.
December 2008

Dr. Laidlaw is a consultant to the State of New Mexico; Thematically Integrated Mathematics Director, Imagine Education Teacher Education Program, Salt Lake City, Utah; and a fourth through ninth grade teacher at Realms of Inquiry, Salt Lake City, Utah.

THE TIME IS RIGHT

While working with the publisher on *Brain-based Teaching for All Subjects* (Rowman and Littlefield Education, 2008), I began to notice comments in the news media about the federal law called No Child Left Behind (NCLB), most likely because it was due for renewal in the fall of 2007. It was originally authorized by President George W. Bush in 2002. I remember a similar focus in 1980 where teachers were trained to emphasize the basic skills students would need to function in the adult world of work. Its aim was "minimum competency testing."

When all was said and done, perhaps minimum competency testing had little effect. A 2002 World Bank publication (Young 2002, p. 44f.) quotes a statistic from the Organization for Economic Co-operation and Development (OECD):

> The United States has a significant problem because more than 45% of the population functions at low literacy (on the OECD scale). Included at this low level are persons with very poor skills who, for example, may not be able to determine from information printed on a package the correct amount of medicine to give a child . . . and only perform tasks that are not too complex.

With NCLB act up for renewal in 2007, people in the educational world were again taking stock.

Some Were Left Behind

One might ask, did No Child Left Behind leave some behind? Based on writings found in newspapers and popular periodicals, you might think so.

Alex Altman (*Time,* June 30, 2008, p. 18) reported "well below average" ranking for U.S. math and graduation rates in two international education comparisons of student achievement made in 2007. Some critics questioned whether the school calendar of 180 days has a deleterious effect on learning and retention. This was not a new idea. Altman mentions Horace Mann's attempt in the 1840s to combine the urban school calendar, usually forty-eight weeks of study, with the rural calendar's summer and winter terms, and scheduling long vacations for agriculture's labor demands.

School calendars continue to be a topic for debate. Critics argue both sides, some citing summer vacation as time to accommodate internships for teens. Some have recommended year-round schools for improved learning when students must meet mandated scores on standardized tests. Others look to teacher accountability.

NCLB test scores are used to rate schools and to consider teacher effectiveness. Some states and large city school systems have considered linking teacher accountability to student achievement. I have always questioned using a student achievement test score as a way of determining teacher accountability because teaching influences so many aspects of students' lives, other than what pupils remember in order to pass a test. Why do we read so much into numbers?

Numbers are in our genetic makeup. Children's brains seem to be wired to pick up the idea of a number line simply because they learn the concept of adding another block to the tower, or taking it away. One of the earliest means of organizing things in the barter and trading system of ancient societies was to develop a counting system for recordkeeping. When you counted something, you were usually sure of what you had. It is a rational goal to want to measure the effectiveness of the American educational system and make improvements where necessary. On the other hand, opponents of NCLB complained bitterly.

What Is Lost in the Counting?

The June 4, 2007, issue of *Time* stated, "'The scope of education isn't supposed to be based on what's tested; it's the other way around,' says P. David Pearson, dean of the University of California, Berkeley, graduate school of education. 'Never send a test out to do a curriculum's job,' he says" (Wallis and Steptoe, pp. 38–39). Test scores are too narrow a scope. And when test scores count so much in school ratings, teachers have to teach toward test topics. This, too, has its critics.

Before the interminable primary stage narrowed the slate in the 2008 presidential election, one of the hopefuls, Governor Michael Huckabee of Arkansas, was quoted in the *New Yorker* for December 3, 2007:

> We have to change and reform the education system so that we're cap-turing both the left and the right sides of the kids' brains. . . . There ought to be a new focus not just in math and science—which there needs to be—but also a balanced focus on music and art and right-side-of-the-brain activities. Otherwise we end up with an education system that's like a data download—a great database but no processor (Hertzberg, p. 36).

The Wallis and Steptoe article in the June 4, 2007, issue of *Time* was titled "Education Special Report: How to Fix No Child Left Behind" (pp. 34–41). The provocative headline suggested something was wrong. The writers described a last-ditch effort to avoid a failing school rating based on test scores, but at what cost? They argued:

> But the decline of science and social studies is often much steeper in schools struggling to end a record of failure. At Arizona Desert El-ementary in San Luis, Ariz., students spend three hours of their 6 1/2 hr. day on literacy and 90 min. on arithmetic. Science is no longer taught as a stand-alone subject. "We had to find ways to embed it within the content of reading, writing and math," says principal Rafael Sanchez, with some regret. Social studies is handled the same way. . . . The school went from failing in 2004 to making AYP (adequate yearly progress) and earning a high-flying "performing plus" designation by the Arizona Department of Education last year (pp. 38–39).

Later in the same article, the writers remind us, "But reading about science isn't the same as incubating chick eggs and watching them hatch. And cutting out field trips to Civil War sites and museums to drill social studies vocabulary words is not the way to build a love of history. Hands-on activities are, for many kids, the best part of school, the part that keeps them engaged" (p. 39). Other journalists cite additional sacrifices made because of the importance of test scores, but all who have been students or educators know that learning is more fun and meaningful when we are actively involved in the process.

Tests Don't Keep School Interesting

In *Newsweek*'s issue for February 11, 2008, Roxana Popescu wrote, "When No Child Left Behind became law in 2002, teachers suspected there'd be some casualties—they just didn't think field trips would be one of them" (p. 12). In the same vein, in a letter, "Let Teachers Use Their Minds," to the editors of the *Washington Post* (July 7, 2007) the writer said, "We know that students are more likely to stay in school when their intellect is engaged and challenged. It should come as no surprise, then, that the same is true for teachers."

But I wasn't prepared to read about a school that missed the No Child Left Behind goals for three years in a row. The *Washington Post Magazine* (April 13, 2008) included an article by Jay Mathews, "The Wrong Yardstick," which described a school that seems to have excellent things taking place. It was doing everything right, but it failed to meet NCLB requirements.

A South Arlington (VA) school failed to meet the federal students achievement targets each of the past three years: Principal Marian Hughey-Guy calls all 430 students by name. . . . Few principals are so popular with their teachers. She listens to their ideas, as many principals do, and then astonishes staff members by giving them the green light and helping them over the rough spots. That is how Barcroft [School] developed its signature program, the Leonardo da Vinci Project, which explored the life of that most versatile of Italian artists through the school's science, math, literature, art and music classes. . . . Who would want to miss the author visits and trips to Jamestown and da Vinci fairs and book exchanges? (p. 23)

It was unfortunate, and ironic, that a school would miss the NCLB score for making progress when parents, teachers, and students were so happy there. Could it be that interesting school experiences might *not* transfer to test scores?

Other Concomitant Problems

Despite its laudable goals, No Child Left Behind was weighed in the balance and found wanting. Mothers in a mid-Atlantic state observed the levels of stress on young children as a result of persistent emphasis on the tests (Blackwell 2008). Another parent complained about wasting time reviewing familiar material from previous grades simply because it would be on the test that year (Glazer 2007).

It was not just lost field trips, lost curricular areas like arts and music, physical education, and even social studies and science. Additional expenses were incurred for the costs of the tests to school systems, resulting in a large profit made from the more than 11.3 million reading and math tests added over the past two years in twenty-three states ("Your Money," 2007). One could ask, was it all worth it?

Some critics spoke of the way the testing emphasis affected electives and even critical thinking (Schambier 2007, p. 3); they point to the way testing affects the ability of schools to provide appropriate placement for individual students' developmental levels. Many gifted students are actually falling behind (Robbins 2007, p. 19).

Creative Teachers Find Solutions

Teachers are finding ways to integrate SOL requirements for more interest and efficiency in teaching; for example, using the SOL standard for current events to create an occasion to learn about another SOL standard, writing business letters, which are then addressed to their senators about important issues.

On May 28, 2008, the broadcast of the *NewsHour* focused on the 2007 New York State Teacher of the Year, Marguerite Izzo, showing her classroom where fifth grade students were lying on their backs, painting the bottoms of their desks to experience what Michelangelo felt as he painted the Sistine Chapel ceiling. A visit to the website of the periodical

New York Teacher brings up an article that mentions how Ms. Izzo uses "history-themed books to help her integrate social studies concepts" ("The Most Important Job").

Good teachers, memorable teachers, beloved teachers, respected teachers are creating ways to keep the Latin verb *educare*—the leading out of student minds into the world of the universe, from the personal toward infinity—in their teaching. Brain research suggests that students learn best in social settings when they are engaged directly in experiences and activities that allow them to *live* what they need to learn. This is a call for integrated, thematic teaching.

History Reminds Us of Past Lessons

In the aftermath of the Industrial Revolution, the three Rs were drilled in order to have a workforce with a third grade literacy level for every child, as recommended by Thomas Jefferson. That level is not enough for the twenty-first century's demands. It is time to embrace a way of teaching that has been woven into or taken out of the pendulum swings between progressive education and traditional schooling, or back-to-basics. We need to connect separate subjects through overarching themes, an idea from the past that will never go away because the brain is structured for it.

Horace Mann's name is forever connected to starting the first real thrust for public education in the United States back in the early nineteenth century. John Dewey and his "learn to do by doing" led to the unit method, which flourished in the early to mid-twentieth century. Remember having a unit on Community Helpers in the first grade? Remember studying the American Indian (Native Americans) in third grade? Yet the book *Why Johnny Can't Read* (Flesch 1955) returned our emphasis to phonics when the whole-word method came into question.

When economic times seem threatened, we look to our schools to produce capable people, leaders of genius in various needed fields. That was our reaction to Russia's launching of Sputnik in 1957. Why were its scientists so far ahead of ours? As a result of this panic, we put the experts in fields of mathematics, social studies, and elsewhere to the work of rethinking content in whatever discipline was being reorganized.

The idea was to aim for the way career people would use that knowledge. We needed to catch up to the Russians. The New Mathematics

Study Group (NMSG) gave us "new math" in the 1960s when the social studies experts gave us Jerome Bruner's "Man: A Course of Study" (MACOS). Teachers were retrained in these new approaches in college courses and workshops.

Edgar Dale developed a "Cone of Experience" (online, 1960) to suggest the varying options for using active learning in the classroom. The broadest slice of the cone, the base, represented real-world experiences, followed by contrived, then dramatized experiences, demonstrations, and field trips to see exhibits, view motion pictures, listen to recordings, or look at photos, pictures, and visual symbols. Testing was at the apex of the cone, the last and smallest element. The more senses involved in the experience, the more effective was the learning, hence the broad base.

Dr. Dale is probably more remembered for his calculations of the amount of learning incurred from different activities. He said people generally remember only 10 percent of what they read, 20 percent of what they hear, 30 percent of what they see, but up to 50 percent of what they both hear and see (videos). When students say (that is, explain) or write what they know, they remember 70 percent, and winning the jackpot is the combination of speaking while doing something; that keeps 90 percent of the material in mind. More of Dale's ideas can be found at www.sjsu.edu/depts/it/itcdpdf/dale.pdf.

Yet in twenty or more years, we were off again, wondering why students graduating from high school weren't prepared for jobs in the marketplace, and we tried the Minimum Competency Testing program.

In contrast, it was noticed that gifted students needed help to reach their potential. The workplace needed young adults better prepared to work in teams and solve problems, to say nothing of graduates who could deal with developing technology's demands. Gifted programs flourished. It was a struggle to keep those programs challenging because most parents wanted the same chances for their children who might not have met the program's entrance criteria. Round and round we went.

Take a Hard Look Today

Now it is time to come around again: to recognize that the testing emphasis has left a lot out of education, especially the arts, physical education, and the fields of social studies and science. Students need to do more than call words when they read, to follow written directions, to learn to use appliances, to fill out forms, or solve basic mathematical problems. They need a background rich in experiences to help them face their complex futures. Thematic teaching has brain-friendly solutions.

A Postscript from China

Questioning the emphasis on test scores is happening all over the world, not only in the United States. An anonymous comment on an online bulletin board, QQ.com, was quoted in the caption beneath a photo from the film *Kung Fu Panda* in the *Washington Post* (Fan 2008). The comment recognized the *authentic* portrayal of Chinese culture in this made-in-Hollywood movie, and wondered why such movies were not being made by the Chinese. The comment read, "If people are educated only to pass exams, then it's very hard to be imaginative. Nowadays, this is an era when people are only stymied by a lack of imagination, not a lack of ability."

Even the Chinese are recognizing that traditional schooling emphasizing tests as evidence of excellence is not enough for the twenty-first century.

By the way, if you need any more reasons to be convinced that thematic teaching is the way to go, check out all the research findings prepared by Naomi Ritter in ERIC document #142 (1999). Thematic teaching wins every time. That is some record!

Winchester, Virginia
Fall 2008

ACKNOWLEDGMENTS

There is a reason why so many spouses are recognized when authors acknowledge and thank people who helped with the long process of publishing a book. Husbands and wives have to accept changes in schedule, deadlines, crises, and reasons for being overlooked at times—all pressures caused by the book-writing process. My husband, James, did not flinch when I told him I was going to write a companion to the first book, and did not noticeably pale when I suggested he might be my reader this time. I continue to give him my undying thanks.

One of the most gratifying experiences of having been a career teacher is to see how students have completed their studies and are contributing now in the adult world. I am indebted to Dr. Scott Laidlaw of Imagine Education for writing the foreword to my book. Scott was a sixth grader when I first knew him, and now he is teaching in one of the most exciting ways, in an integrated curriculum that actively involves students indoors and out. He is also a creator and designer of educational games.

Though referred to in the text as my science, or my science and math, colleague, George C. Craig III was our muse and genius when we worked on the evolution of those five themes for sixth grade based on social studies. I would never have seen sanitized owl pellets as a class experience in archaeological excavation. I accepted no longer having available the Thunderbird Museum of Early Man, but didn't think of having Cave Man Day in the Park as an effective substitute. His mind was creative, innovative, and challenging, and he was a stability factor with his reassuring response, "No problem."

ACKNOWLEDGMENTS

Glenne White and Hartley Schearer, my librarian support system, were invaluable cohorts when the three-year sequential program fostered the themes described in chapters 7 and 8. They were always available for library orientation classes and creating reading lists on various topics, but it was their active participation in working out the curriculum themes by reacting to ideas, seeing weak spots, and suggesting further project-type assignments out of their own vast backgrounds that was a gift beyond measure.

Barbara Sankovich was the art teacher who worked with sixth graders on the African masks, and showed seventh graders how to make the double-sided half-masks for our reading of *The Taming of the Shrew*. She was a true help when she shared her expert's eye to evaluate the students' original responses to the geographical features in the three-media project.

When we moved to Winchester in 1973, we didn't know that a student at the Shenandoah Conservatory of Music would become a lifelong friend and a teacher colleague. When I refer to my colleague in Colorado in the text of this book, I am grateful each time to Roberta Szoka for sharing her enthusiasm and ideas about thematic teaching, as well as what she learned from her experiences.

A septuagenarian grandmother does not expect to have a Facebook page on the Internet, but part of the bolstering of my determination to write this book came from my former students. Now a middle school teacher herself, Amy Costello Wilfong started a group on Facebook, to which another student sent me a link so I could check it out: Everything I Need to Know I Learned from Mrs. Dr. Laster. I was alternately overwhelmed, thrilled, and then proud to find out what my former students were doing to make this world a better place. The way they were succeeding, perhaps we did something right in middle school.

Two technologically gifted friends from the younger generation have been irreplaceable experts, producing what I could not: the graphic files for the books' illustrations, and the website existing in cyberspace, with the Bulletin Board and Teachers' Lounge pages, at www.madlonlaster .com. Thank you, Angela Lee of Leeway Graphic Design, and thank you, Andrew Napier. Angie's artistic judgment is unfailing (leewaygraphic design.com); Andrew is my valuable and amazing computer consultant (www.designnapier.com).

A faculty colleague at the middle school, and now a faculty member at our regional community college, Dr. Kate Simpson has been an encouraging cheerleader who even offered to read a draft of the manuscript without being asked. No one succeeds in projects without support from colleagues like Kate. No wonder friendships are treasured over the years.

Again I thank Tom Koerner and Maera Winter at Rowman and Littlefield Education for accepting my second manuscript for publication. I have enjoyed working with them on this, my second book.

THE BRAIN IS WIRED
TO FILE BY ASSOCIATION

"Mommy, when did I lose my first tooth?"

"Don't you remember, sweetie? We were at the park when your cousins were visiting. We had a picnic; Daddy grilled chicken, and we had corn on the cob."

"Oh, yes! I do remember! I took a big bite, and my front tooth came out. I almost swallowed it. It was the same size as a kernel of corn. I can still remember that I tasted blood for a little while. That was yucky. It was so hot; and that was the day Susie broke her arm falling off the jungle gym."

People who are contestants on game shows are whizzes at remembering discrete bits of information: dates, cities, winners of World Series games, names of famous people—the kind of facts cognitive scientists call declarative information. We also remember ways of doing things: called procedural knowledge. We generalize what we learn about shopping at a small neighborhood store as opposed to huge, syndicated department stores from national chains, which sell merchandise in many categories and have multiple checkout lanes.

We learn to purchase food differently at fast food establishments with both drive-up windows and inside seating, as opposed to "white tablecloth restaurants" with tuxedoed waiters and famous chefs. We are always trying new places to eat, but we have a general sense of how to operate within the system for a particular type of restaurant. We remember what happened in each restaurant and create an *average* or generalized memory to apply to new eating places. We master the concept of what the term *restaurant* means.

We have specific memories too, details we can recall because they were very memorable experiences: the night the crepe suzettes flamed so near the smoke alarms that the fire company responded. Given the memory of the surprised faces of the firemen when they arrived at the restaurant and found the flaming dessert had affected the ceiling sensors, we might remember exactly what we had ordered that evening, what we were celebrating, and with whom. The emotional overlay of the episode of the flaming pancakes seared, in a way, the memory into our brains.

People help each other with memory retrieval. The child who forgot when he lost his tooth is reminded of the park picnic by his mother, and he immediately recalls other elements of the situation. He might even recall something his mother did not. But when left alone with elusive information we can't immediately retrieve, we all have other ways to *strain the brain* and locate in our mental files what we want to remember.

When you know a first name for someone but cannot remember the last, you can sometimes recall it if you bring to mind the situation where you saw them last. Images of settings, other people in attendance, topics of conversation will all begin to rattle those recalcitrant neurons until the last name pops into your frontal lobes, and you have it. Sometimes it takes longer than a few seconds or minutes. The older you are, the more you might joke about the bit of information arriving the next morning after your mental secretary searched the files all night during your sleep. It is okay if the name is found.

Other information stays in our memories, almost unbidden, because they conjure up a fearful situation. E-mails circulate with alarming reports of personal experiences with criminals. Women are encouraged to take self-defense classes, but also to notice their surroundings. One particular e-mail warned about putting groceries in your car.

You might notice a piece of paper stuck on the windshield when you get in to drive away. Seeing the paper, you get out of the car while leaving your keys in the ignition. In that brief moment, a carjacker jumps into the driver's seat and takes off, leaving you with a scrap of paper in your hand. Women reading such warnings hope that, every time they are finished shopping and loading purchases into the car, the setting will remind them to be cautious. We need to avoid instilling fear in students. We have other ways to help them retain information. But emotional overlays make learning stronger; it is true.

A lot of what we know about the way the brain learns and remembers is based on general observations we make while we are around growing children. When children begin to talk, they learn the names, or labels, for the things in their environment, most likely starting with Mama or Mommy since it is easier to begin with the lips together and turn them into the *M*-sound than to master the muscle skill to create a *D*-sound for Dada or Daddy. Try that, and compare *M*-sounds with *D*-sounds to see what is involved.

Today, there is brain research to back up our folk knowledge. And we know scientists can check a baby in its first month of life and know whether the infant can discern between the sound of the letter *P* and that of *B* (Molfese, n.d.; Kluger 2008). Scientists can tell then if a child will have reading difficulties by the age of eight. But, most of all, brain researchers know that when a stimulus is presented to a subject in a research study, neural activity shows up in several areas simultaneously, networking.

A toddler sees a dog, and parents say, "See the doggie?" After another sighting or two of a domesticated canine, the child's brain has stored a visual pattern to differentiate *dog* from *cat*. Gradually she learns that dogs have names, are pets, and that some dogs might be homeless and not safe to approach. Items like doghouses, collars, dog food, toys, bones, treats, and flea powder might all be stored in something like a semantic network, a knowledge system for *dogs*. When the child has later experiences with dogs, other associations with *dog* will be added, like names for species and mixed breeds, veterinarian visits, and tricks dogs learn.

Donald Norman diagrammed these related concepts as semantic networks (1982, pp. 45–50). The basic concept, perhaps *birds*, was written in a circle, and associated information in other circles was connected to the original, and often to other associated information, by solid lines. Because each stored concept has situations, labels or terms, and the sounds of the labels (audio or spoken memory) attached to the original idea, information is stored in associated networks. Failing to recall one bit of information usually leads a person to renew the search from another direction within that network.

To repeat a quote from *Brain-based Teaching for All Subjects: Patterns to Promote Learning,* "As early as 1982, Donald Norman stated: 'My belief is that visual memory serves the later stages of processing by maintaining an image for a sufficient length of time to let those stages do their jobs'" (Laster 2008, p. 9). *Stages* is a term that refers to adding related information that gives further dimension to the original concept. Learning is definitely lifelong. Watching the *Westminster Dog Show* on television when in your fifties, you reference a mental connection initially established when you were a toddler.

Experiences construct patterns and promote learning throughout our lives, no matter how long we live. What teachers need to do is establish the basic concepts of the curricula as images, as patterns in the minds of their students, and then use that initially constructed concept to add associated information through further learning experiences. The more children are involved in what they are learning, the more they remember, the better the memory is stored, and the more efficiently this information is retrieved.

Child-care centers, preschools, and kindergartens have their kitchen corners, dress-up boxes, and play stores. Teachers of all ages have used varied strategies to reach the students in their classrooms: in the 1970s, learning centers were used in some classrooms. Other strategies include hands-on crafts and projects, dramatizations, field trips, literature groups, science experiments, music and art activities, small groups tackling topics together, even independent study projects. Various trends appeared over time; teachers tried them, and kept what worked successfully, and, when other teaching trends showed up, they didn't abandon everything *old* for a *new* idea.

It is probably unfortunate that we have the term *bag of tricks*, since a trick is a false impression, a twist on the truth for the purpose of entertaining, or gentle coercion, but certainly not a proper educational term. If we can get past the idea of tricking students into learning, and consider classroom activities as the *strategies* to get them to learn (a term I associate with the 1980s), we will at least tempt students into learning, sometimes without their knowing they have done so.

When we meet students, years later, who are adults and out of school, they may recall activities done in our classes. I think I can safely say that what they remember is never the way they were trained for the mandated tests required by the state or the federal government. Although it could be—if you had trained them with crazy mnemonic devices, or catchy songs about chemistry found in an ancient copy of *Mad Magazine* that you saved for decades. I'll allow myself to admit that much.

When General McArthur was relieved of his command by President Truman during the Korean War (1950–1953), his farewell speech gave American English a quotable statement that is still with us over half a century later: "Old soldiers never die; they just fade away."

Some teaching ideas never die, but they do fade to the point where they seem to be preserved in corners of the classrooms of career teachers nearing retirement. Students in those classrooms still get to experience the *tried and true*, and usually become excited about some topic or other. But the testing emphasis raised its head yet again at the end of the twentieth century, and in the twenty-first century, federal and state mandated tests have changed what happens in schools, dramatically in most cases. (The proof is not in the pudding, but in the preface of this book.)

Thematic teaching is a tried-and-true idea that lives on at websites in cyberspace, some classrooms, and in the memories of teachers who swore by it in their careers. Themes link related ideas, materials, and skills the same way the brain links related concepts and associations with basic ideas in the neural wiring of our gray matter. We are bucking Mother Nature by overlooking this medically researched and proven situation. I still say that we teachers ignore brain research at our peril.

Horace Mann wanted a literate workforce for the factories of the nineteenth century; John Dewey knew twentieth-century children would learn what they needed to for their adult lives if they were allowed to have direct experiences: "to learn to do by doing" was his slogan. Jerome Bruner was impressed by the Russian theorist Lev Vygotsky's work with children's language development and its relationship to internal speech or thought (Vygotsky 1962). That was coupled with Jean Piaget's observations of child development leading to his stage theory (Sprenger 1999, pp. 6–7).

Bruner (1962) realized that children were exposed to the same concepts over and over again in their lives, and learned more from each repeated experience due to maturity levels they had achieved. He developed his theory of a *spiral curriculum* where he asserted a child could be taught anything at any age as long as it was taught in a developmentally appropriate way.

Our brains are attracted to ideas by their novelty, color, appearance—where closed shapes are preferred or noticed more quickly than script—sound, and motion. They learn best in social situations through experiences involving them directly. They continually add information to concepts and associations already stored in memory. Memories are fixed more firmly when more than one sensory pathway is involved. And even though we talk about visual learners or kinesthetic learners, or even audio learners, we all initially store a concept visually, attaching other sensory experiences to that model.

Thematic teaching involves all of the senses in establishing concepts, and creates many more neural connections simply because of the subject matter integration involved with classroom activities. It is the way to go.

While integrating and correlating areas of study under overarching themes is brain friendly—in that it imitates the way the brain stores what it chooses on its own—my personal opinion is that thematic teaching works best at elementary and middle school levels. One might think that integrated curricula would occur effortlessly at the high school level. Yet a high school student, on a panel I heard, complained about being put off by her history teacher when she asked a question relating to something she'd learned in art class. She was told, "Wait till next week when we get to that topic."

At the high school level, it may be a better solution to simply schedule class topics at the same time in two or more courses, and build associations directly into the class material. More limitations seem to exist at the secondary level, and the requirements work against full integration of the disciplines. Speakers, writers, print materials all assume readers have basic information learned from their schooling. Societies function more smoothly when shared cultural information is understood by each citizen (Hirsch 1987).

Overarching themes shared by two or three disciplines might be directly related for the most part, but if a British literature course requires specific book titles and authors, it might be hard to ensure students don't leave that course without having met and mastered those sources. What they did read fit the theme, but certain authors deemed a *must* might be skirted or overlooked entirely. Relate where you can, but produce well-trained student scholars who exit high schools prepared for undergraduate studies, or the job market.

Now fix yourself a cup of tea or coffee, or whatever you sit down to sip in the teachers' lounge, and imagine that you asked me what exciting things might be going on in my classroom. These chapters will tell you.

"Interdisciplinary learning is a process closer to the way the human brain is naturally designed to learn best" —Eric Jensen, 1995

YOU DON'T HAVE TO GO WHOLE HOG AT THE BEGINNING

Teaching is a daunting career: your responsibilities in the present are innumerable; your influence on the future is monumental. While it may sound trite and dismissive to say teaching is never boring, I can honestly say that teaching can be more fun than the proverbial barrel of monkeys. Teachers who have goals in mind and find a creative path to reach them find themselves challenged, able to use their imaginations and maintain their own intellectual curiosity. You, too, can actually look forward to going to school every day for the rest of your career.

Let's put the emphasis on the creative and the intellectually curious parts.

Pay Attention to Your Own Thinking Processes

You can gently ease yourself into teaching where you use overarching themes that represent the content of the curriculum. I am sure I didn't purposefully plan to integrate English and social studies when I began teaching sixth grade in Nashville, Tennessee, in 1961. The plan book pages for the week were empty in front of me, and we were starting a chapter on ancient Greece in the social studies book. Our local schools still provide standard-issue plan books. The concept of ancient Greece is inexorably tied to Greek myths in my brain. I discovered myths right after feeding my fascination for worldwide folktales when I was about six or seven.

I wrote down the social studies chapter and pages, some notes on what we would do, and filled in "read myths" under the planning blocks for reading. I may have noted "write an original myth" under English composition. That was my beginning. I'm fairly sure I only thought in terms of social studies information from the textbook chapter plus reading some classic myths. I probably didn't think of *kourambeides*, the buttery Greek shortbread cookies with chopped nuts—pistachios or walnuts. I'd been to Athens and had slides of the Acropolis to share.

Of course it was natural to proceed to the next chapter on ancient Rome and remember that the Romans had a pantheon that merged with that of the Greeks when the Romans conquered them. We could read more myths and learn new Roman names for the gods and goddesses. I just fell into the pattern of widening the social studies topic with whatever connected naturally, meaning whatever occurred to *me* at the time. I was also blessed with an older colleague, and we used to plan together so students didn't compare what they were doing or not doing in our separate classrooms when they were riding the school buses together. What a mentor she turned out to be, and I had taught five years already.

What Comes to Mind?

I may have just given you the first approach to thematic teaching, which is like the song from the Broadway musical *Annie Get Your Gun*, "Doin' What Comes Natur'lly"!

You have a topic or a theme you need to teach. What comes up naturally in your educated mind that you associate with that topic? Can you do that in your classroom? If you are in a self-contained classroom situation, whether you do your own art and music or not, you really have control of just how much you want to coordinate the subjects. Start small and broaden your reach as you become comfortable crossing subject lines with the same theme.

Solo or Whole School?

You can start, in your own classroom, by combining two subjects like social studies and reading, as Greece and mythology were linked. The opposite end of the continuum is possible as well. Sometimes whole schools have correlated their lessons, no matter what the subject.

While we were living in the faculty apartments on a campus in Beirut, Lebanon, a British couple lived across the hall. The husband had taught in a British grammar school in the Midlands where the headmaster posted, on the academic calendar in the teachers' lounge, the themes or topics and the dates when they would be the focus. Teachers planned lessons on those topics for those days or weeks, and it didn't involve a lot of meetings or much overt cooperation.

Each teacher made his or her own individual effort, but students knew if they were reading a book about mountain climbing in English, they might be studying various geographical regions in social studies class, and considering geology topics like the types of rock in science—sedimentary, igneous, and metamorphic. Plate tectonics and the earth's crust make another natural focus. Health classes could deal with the consequences of the Incas of Peru in South America living at such high altitudes in the Andes. How did athletes train for the Olympic Games held in Mexico when the plateau was four thousand feet altitude or more?

Math students could practice some challenging arithmetical processes when the comparative heights of peaks in the Himalayas were subtracted from each other. The class could compile a graph to represent the results visually. A timeline of who climbed which record-breaking mountain peak in what year would certainly open up a sport not publicized regularly for all to know. Rock climbing is a more familiar hobby, and students could be introduced to the thrills and dangers, and the need to be trained, if they heard a presentation from a visitor to their classroom.

Fiction books like *Banner in the Sky*, a Newbery Honor Book by James Ramsey Ullman, give accounts of mountain climbing—in this case, in the Swiss Alps. Biographies of climbers who have tackled Mt. Everest and K-2 would produce terrific book reports in any of a variety of formats. High school students might tackle the opening chapters of Greg Mortenson's *Three Cups of Tea* to learn how the author almost lost his life from oxygen deprivation and found his life's work building schools to provide opportunities for children in mountain villages of Afghanistan and Pakistan.

Making connections can become too contrived, as in having the music teacher teach yodeling, but mountain songs from various parts of the world would be appropriate, especially ones with regional references, like Norwegian and Swiss hiking songs. Focus on what is valuable. The art teacher might be involved in some natural way: painting landscapes? Art history and appreciation lessons could bring in the landscapes of the Hudson River School (Robinson 1988) or the museum quality photos of Ansel Adams, a pioneer in black and white landscape photography in the twentieth century. You can display books on tables and use today's ready-made PowerPoint presentations available in school catalogues.

There you have the two extremes: correlating your various lessons within the self-contained classroom, or agreeing to teach appropriate content in your subject area at the same time the rest of the faculty address the same topic from their discipline's perspective. *Correlation* is the term, but it is more like parallel teaching, since in a whole-school effort, timing is more important than cooperative planning. A brainstorming session might be helpful, though, to suggest ideas that might fit under the theme or title of the study.

In this case, the cooperation of a faculty involved in teaching on the same content theme is more important than how each teacher carries out his or her responsibilities.

Don't Rule Out Serendipity

Sometimes resources just fall into your lap. When my cousin was active in her sons' school, she gave me a copy of *Keepers of the Earth: Native American Stories and Environmental Activities for Children* (Caduto and Bruchac 1988).

A marvelous section, chapter 8, is rich with information about rocks. It begins with a story from the Lakota/Sioux tribes of the Great Plains, "Tunka-Shila, Grandfather Rock," followed by "Old Man Coyote and the Rock," from the Pawnee on the Great Plains. There is a background essay on rock sources, with questions about the stories. But there is a gem of an activity called "Rock to Rock: A Fantasy Journey," where students close their eyes and listen to the teacher read the prompt that begins:

> Imagine that you are a rock as big as a baseball. Your home is on a sunny hillside, and you can see down into a deep valley with a river roaring below. . . . Can you feel the sunlight warming you?

Descriptions follow for two other activities involving drawing and labeling rocks, and pantomiming, and then there is a suggestion for extending the experience with an investigation of soil. Any student would develop ideas about rocks and soil before getting to science class.

Some Students Make Their Own Connections

In the introduction, I mentioned attending a conference and hearing a panel of four high school students discuss the ways they coped in heterogeneous classrooms. A bright young girl told of her frustration when she asked a question about a historic period, the focus of her art class, but asked the question in her history class. She had made the natural connection. The teacher put her off and told her to ask her question the next week when they would cover that chapter.

Bright students may make connections and ask questions more readily than other students, but all students will have crossover revelations because of the way the mind stores learned information. Correlating eases and actually encourages the process, as does activating the prior knowledge students already have stored in their minds. Start with what they know and build on that.

A self-contained classroom gives teachers leeway as to when and how much correlation they create. During my teaching years in Tennessee, classrooms were self-contained to the max, as they say. If art and music happened, the teacher made them happen. They could go on a tangent as well, with a good reason, of course. Those were the days of not too much control and a lot of classroom variety. Schools did have a standardized testing program scheduled once a year in the spring, however. A cumulative record card demonstrated the results across a student's school career. Systemwide testing was not ignored, but not stressed either. It was simply scheduled like an annual overall report card.

This was the decade when schooling was labeled as teacher centered or child centered. Since the teacher remains the adult in charge even in a child-centered classroom, there is more to be said about the two approaches. But there are times when taking the lead from your students is the wise thing to do. On a cultural exchange tour to the Far East, I became fascinated by Japan. I found a book by Phyllis Whitney, in the school library, called *The Secret of the Samurai Sword*. It involved a ghost in a Japanese garden and a travel writer's two grandchildren. While reading it aloud to the class after lunch, or after a half-hour recess as a calming practice, I found they were hooked on Japanese culture too.

Soon we learned to sing the well-known "Cherry Blossom Song" in English and Japanese, and did *origami*, the paper-folding technique developed centuries ago. We wrote the seventeen-syllable *haiku* poetry. But the students were fifth graders, and visitors to the classroom would comment, "I didn't know you studied Japan in the fifth grade." No one actually objected, though. Students were involved with a variety of activities focused on one theme, and wasn't that our goal? The more students learn of other cultures, the more understanding we can have in the world, building more respect for others and an appreciation for how they choose to live.

Enlist Help

Correlation is still possible with traveling teachers you see regularly but not daily for art and music classes, or with teachers in art and music who are in the same building with you but are too busy to do extra planning. Sometimes the teachers of art and music are devoted to the concepts they want or need to treat within their own curriculum. Other times they are happy to insert something new that relates to your curriculum theme. Even art and music teachers become a bit tired of the same old stuff. Check with these talented people whose fields make life worth living. They usually want students to love learning and their subject areas as much as you do.

As Dr. Joyce VanTassel-Baska of the College of William and Mary once stated at a conference, "Don't forget the arts." Bringing in art, music, and drama, even dance, feeds intellectual curiosity, taps creativity, brings out innate abilities, and inspires students beyond just making more mental neuron pathways. You might open up a child's future as well as his mind.

Lean on the Librarian: Become an Academic Team

My mother, a seventeen-year veteran of a first grade classroom, recommended finding allies in the school secretary and the custodian. I am sure she probably felt the same way about the school librarian, though she purchased many books for her own classroom bookshelves.

Do not try to operate a curriculum where you are linking subject areas under a shared topic without working closely with your school's librarian. This is even more important with schools' home pages becoming a portal to information sources beyond imagination. You save time and energy because the librarian-media specialist will know that particular collection of tomes, and will be another creative mind with which to bandy about ideas, judging their worth, their potential, the materials available to support the activity or topic, and the visual aids that abound in this technologically wired world. That colleague can be a source of wonderful advice and know-how. Become an academic team; you will have more fun, too.

Social Studies Really Is a Great Ally

In a self-contained classroom, you effectively team with yourself. Themes do not have to come from social studies, although you reinforce more difficult concepts when you build associations on a framework of history.

Early grades used to begin a social studies curriculum called "Expanding Communities," where the youngest students talked about their families and families around the world. Next, the focus enlarged to include "Community Helpers." Native Americans were always a third grade unit, whereas fourth grade studied the biomes, the geographic regions like hot wetlands, hot drylands, temperate zones, and the frigid zones at the poles. By the time they got to fifth grade, the emphasis was on their home state and how it fit into U.S. history.

With a composite understanding of families in societies living in different ways around the globe, based on the climate and geography, students understood U.S. history better when they learned it started with the ambitions and dreams of Christopher Columbus and the explorers, followed by the trading vessels dealing in spices, and finally those settling new lands for one reason or another. A private school in Virginia teaches world history before U.S. history so that students see how events in Europe and elsewhere affected our early centuries, and in later centuries, incoming groups of immigrants. That is another example of seeing the whole before focusing on one of the parts.

Eventually most schools immersed sixth grade in the history of the Eastern Hemisphere, returned to the Western Hemisphere in seventh grade, and took basic looks at economics, government, and geography in the eighth grade. The focus started with the individual student and expanded to the whole world, geographically and historically. Within that social studies emphasis, we can find just about any theme we need, whether related to history and geography, or just emanating from it.

Feed the Always Hungry

Do not forget feeding the hungry. *Kourambeides*, the Greek shortbread, was mentioned above along with the topic of ancient Greece. Students of most ages love to fix food, either at school or at home, to bring it in for class snacks. It might be less than convenient at the high school level, but feasting during class (a medieval banquet) or nibbling on typical finger food from a particular country, region, or culture is a way to widen the horizons of your students. They certainly become involved.

Eating ethnic yummies has another advantage for students. They notice that typical preparations and means for cooking or baking probably stem from the resources and geography of the region or nation, as do the ingredients. Parents report that their children are more willing to try things at restaurants as the result. Food is such a personal thing, that experiencing it is another window into a different culture.

Touch Other Areas Obliquely

Math isn't a subject that is totally removed from correlating with other areas in education. A substitute teacher, finishing the year for a colleague who left for National Guard service, introduced the idea of *palindromes* in math class. Palindromes in our English language are intriguing: words and even clauses that read the same in both directions—forward or reverse. *Level* and *radar* are palindromes, but so is that reference to President Teddy Roosevelt: *A man, a plan, a canal, Panama!*

When the substitute teacher introduced palindromes in math class, it involved columns of numerals and noting when a number is reached that has the same numerals in position going forward or in reverse, as in 202 or 1881, or 321,123. She was introducing patterns and such in our decimal system. She suggested telling the students about palindromes in English. So be it. This was a short-term theme, but it sparked interest.

Later I discovered a school book club order, offering a paperback of cartoons illustrating various funny and idiotic palindromes. It was Allan Miller's *Mad Amadeus Sued a Madam*. The title is a palindrome in itself. That is one to titillate you. "Mustafa's tent nets a fat sum" is another. Can you not see that this aspect of language might appeal to certain ages of students, say middle and high school, just in passing? Students might create one or two of their own, accepting the unspoken challenge. Do give extra credit on their grade averages if the subject of their creations connects with the curriculum.

Vary Activities to Meet Individual Needs; Play Games

Is a student a kinesthetic learner—learning things with his or her hands—or is the student an audio learner, or a visual learner? Teachers were guided by the idea of a preferred style of learning, followed it for a while, and still bring it to the fore now and then. The more varied the activities involved with a topic or theme, the better. Several catalogues for children's toys offer products that foster learning, thinking, hobbies, and other interests. They are good sources for games that involve students with the same information they are learning in their textbooks.

The principal may arrive at your door to say, "You can't have them sitting around all period playing games!" Don't be cowed. Try having a game day and invite the principal to visit the class. Plan to introduce one game or a few pertinent to the theme or topic, and then invite those students who are interested to come in and play them after school, with a note of permission from the parent, of course. If students ride school buses, after school activities that aren't on a regular schedule can be too daunting to arrange. Just use the old learning center idea in your classroom. If you do have a game day, invite the parents to look in as well as the principal.

Introduce a game to the whole class at once; then send groups of two, three, or four, as the case might be, to the game table in the back corner during class time. Rotate the playing of the game through the class until all have had a chance to play. A game that does not take too long to play gives you an advantage, but sometimes even a partial experience with a game is of value. It whets the appetite for more. Then you might have students asking to come in after school, and they will arrange their own transportation and bring other classmates as players. They might ask Santa for the game.

Here are some games with educational value, some traditional over centuries, all published in the twentieth century. One or two may no longer be available; at least they are examples of possibilities that might be on the market now. If you search the Internet for Aristoplay, you'll find it is still a viable game source for the twenty-first century. Others may be also. And check museum shops and their catalogues. Check catalogues for children's toys as well. This list starts with a game connected with ancient Greece:

- *By Jove: A Game and a Book of Classical Adventure.* Ann Arbor, MI: Aristoplay, 1983. For two to six players, ages ten and up.

- *Civilization: Game of the Heroic Age.* The Dawn of History, 8000 B.C. to 250 B.C. A Book Case Game. Baltimore: The Avalon-Hill Game Company, 1982. For two to seven players, ages twelve and up.

- *Conquest of the Empire: Second Century Rome.* Milton-Bradley Gamemaster Series. Springfield, MA: Milton-Bradley Company, 1984. For two to six players, ages ten to adult.

- *Expedition: A Game of Archaeological Adventure and Discovery in Egypt.* Janesville, WI: Whitehall Games, Inc., 1980. For two or more players, ages nine to adult.

- *Game of the States: Who Sells the Most from Coast to Coast?* Springfield, MA: Milton-Bradley Company, 1960. For two to four players, ages seven to fourteen.

- *King Tut's Game: Senet.* Chicago: Cadaco, Inc., 1977. For two players, ages ten and up.

- *Parcheesi: Royal Game of India.* Bay Shore, NY: Selchow and Righter, 1982. For four players, ages six to adult.

- *Pilgrimage: A Medieval Game.* Janesville, WI: Whitehall Games, 1984. For two to six players, ages eight to adult.

- *Wild Life: An Ecology Game that Fosters Wild Animal Conservation*. New York: E. S. Lowe Company. For two to five players, ages seven to adult.

- *World Traveler*. Needham, MA: Mr. World Traveler, Ltd., 1980. For six players, ages eight to adult.

Mystery games are a good place to start when teaching the mystery genre in literature, and two games represent the concept well:

- *Clue: Parker Brothers Detective Game*. Beverly, MA: Parker Brothers Div. of General Mills Fun Group. For three to six players, ages eight to adult.

- *The Sherlock Holmes Game*. Chicago: Cadaco, Inc., 1982. For two to four players, ages six and up.

There was a computer simulation game called *Castle: Seige and Conquest* (Irvine, CA: MacPlay, 1992–1993). Technologically speaking, it is hopelessly outdated now, using multiple floppy disks to insert where slots on computers no longer exist for them. But it was an example of historical portrayals, since it began in 1312 A.D./C.E. The computer played four of the five lords after the game player selected the one he or she wished to be.

Several young sixth grade boys came in after school to play the game and managed to create an approach that allowed them to work together at the computer. Small groups allow for learning in a social setting, which keeps the brain happier. *Castle* is probably on a CD now (www.ask .metafilter.com). Google it, and you even find a Wikipedia article for the game.

Other computer games, which may have been updated but are still examples of those that support curricular themes, include these:

- *Amazon Trail*. St. Paul, MN: MECC Games, 1996. For ages nine and up (CD).

- *Sim City*. Walnut Creek, CA: Maxis Games, 1996. For ages six to adults (CD).

- *The Yukon Trail.* St. Paul, MN: MECC Games, 1996. For ages six to sixteen (on floppy disks, 3.25").

- *The Oregon Trail* from MECC Games might also be available.

Enlist student help whenever possible. Two or three students played *Sim City* to see how it went. They thought having the class, as a group, run the city and vote on decisions would work better, but small groups could run a few cities, creating several versions of the game of *Sim City*. *Sim City* is produced by the company Maxis and is available on the Internet.

This chapter now leaves you to your own devices in the quest of thematic teaching. Let it happen.

> *Tell me, I forget.*
> *Show me, I remember.*
> *Involve me, I understand.*

> —*www.todaysteacher.com*

CHAPTER TWO

COORDINATE AND CORRELATE: SCHEDULE AND SHARE

At times I feel that I am truly writing my own career story, sharing with teachers and parents what I found to be the essence of a real education for children passing through our schools. For me, theme teaching was like Topsy, Harriet Beecher Stowe's character "who jus' grew'd" in *Uncle Tom's Cabin*. Situations presented themselves, and I dealt with them.

Education courses teach us about goal-setting, anticipatory-set, guided practice, engaging the students, and evaluation. On the one hand I embraced theme teaching in an open-ended way, but I am not the free-spirit type. I need to be organized, to know where I am going. It may be the adventure of exploration that sold me on theme teaching, more fun than lesson plan books. One idea could take off in marvelous and meaningful directions. Yet it could not be successful without planning and organization.

Responding to a Need

We had been organizing our middle school class groups based on what level students had reached in the reading series they were using. When students came to middle school, we found that we had below level and grade level reading groups, and even advanced groups ready to read the seventh grade book. In an attempt to provide enrichment for students needing a challenge, a colleague—librarian, inveterate traveler, and gourmet cook—suggested that we could offer them something special. That was how Cultures and Cuisines, an after-school exploratory program, was born.

We planned four sessions of cooking that spring: Middle Eastern, Italian, French, and Chinese, and then hosted an International Dinner night, sort of an exotic potluck dinner, as the culminating event. For the next seventeen years, Cultures and Cuisines was a monthly program after school, with an ethnic cooking focus following the social studies curriculum in sixth grade at the time: preparing food that was Middle Eastern and Greek, Italian, French, German, Russian, Indian, Chinese, and Japanese. Here, too, social studies was a handy and logical alliance.

There was a routine: snacks first, then an introduction to the country or region, usually via old-fashioned slides, and then food preparation for the day. While the food cooked, there was an activity—*mah jongg* for China, *backgammon* for the Middle East; one year a mother came and gave a talk on pasta in Italy—and then we ate. Flipping crepes for France and rolling *beureks* from Turkey, or making fresh pasta with a pasta machine were highlights.

Ethnic food is an exceptionally adaptable learning experience for all grade levels. Food prepared at home can be brought in and shared, or cooked in the classroom with safety precautions taken into consideration. Slow cookers do well with dishes like Polish sausage or South American beans. Families with overseas origins can bring or send food to be sampled, or a parent can come and make a presentation. Some foods are simple enough to prepare in the classroom and then take to the school kitchen to bake.

An Administrative Move: Teaching in Tandem

A colleague and I had been on a four-teacher team when our building was brand new. We knew we could plan together. We had correlated informally already. My science colleague taught the universe, planets, and constellations when I was working with the social studies text on ancient Greece and Rome and classical mythology. When the administration returned teachers to two-teacher teams, he suggested we continue using social studies as the foundation of a more integrated curriculum, saying, "You can hang anything on social studies." How many times have I quoted him verbatim on that?

We built on what we had already done over the years when integrating subjects simply by mutual agreement; now we would be formal with a written curriculum. Remember the rule of thumb: at any grade level the class probably has a range of abilities equal to the grade. A heterogeneously grouped fourth grade class would have students across a four-year span of ability levels: a year or two below and a year or so above.

Even with a range of ability levels, we did not change the curriculum we had already written. Interdisciplinary units more nearly reflect life. Related areas are intertwined, and students can see more cause-and-effect relationships. We don't *live* or *think* in separate compartments. Teachers can respond to differences in children more efficiently and effectively when subjects are integrated. Themes reach students in heterogeneously grouped classrooms and in homogeneously assigned classes (see Ritter 1999).

Schools that are scheduled as a traditional junior high have separate classes for separate subjects. That prevents putting groups together easily, or having teachers integrate subjects with the same group at the same time. It is more like parallel teaching, as described in the first chapter. As we have seen, themes can survive in varying situations.

In one such case, in the interest of communication, students took a serious look at television in people's daily lives. While in language arts class, they analyzed program offerings, calculated percentages in various categories, and presented findings from commercial and public TV channels. When they went to science class, they focused on how television worked, the electronics of transmission, and actually produced a school news television program recorded by portable camcorder and viewed on the classroom television set.

More integration was possible when students were part of a two-teacher team consisting of a math-science teacher and a language arts–social studies teacher. As part of the communications theme, students watched a taped news program from one of the commercial channels. They noted the various jobs involved when the credits rolled by. When they wrote letters to persons on the crew asking about their particular jobs, one student received a letter inviting the class to visit the news program's set and stay for a live telecast. That was a perfect opportunity for sixth graders already planning and organizing their own school news show. This will be discussed in more detail in chapter 4.

Today there is more access to good quality video material, and people are able to splice video clips, post them online, and share them with class groups.

Combine for Efficiency and Flexibility

Teaching in the two-teacher team covering the four core subjects gave us more freedom. We could follow the schedule with separate periods for subjects, or we could put the classes together to watch a film in one showing, instead of projecting it twice as the two groups came separately to their classes. During a study of the Middle Ages, a member of a madrigal singing group at our local university's conservatory came after school one day and taught a small group the "Earl of Salisbury's Pavane." The students involved planned on performing this at the medieval banquet we had scheduled.

The art teacher helped seventh graders prepare for a reading of Shakespeare's *The Taming of the Shrew* during a theme called "Conflict and Resolution" (discussed in chapter 7). She showed students how to make the Mardi Gras ball half-masks, held on a dowel in front of the face but moved for ease of reading. When a student read a role where the character was disguised to be someone else as part of the plot, the mask was constructed so both sides could represent different roles: Hortensio disguised himself as a music teacher to have access to Bianca and woo her for himself. The same art teacher helped in evaluating projects involving artistic materials and ideas. Her expertise was appreciated.

Creative Applications

There was a lot of serendipity involved when the science department chairman ordered sanitized owl pellets for the sixth grade classes to pull apart to discover tiny mouse bones from an owl's nightly repast. That undoubtedly created a vivid image supported by the memory of the predator bird's diet and habits. My colleague and I arrived in the parking lot at the same time the day after the post delivered the pellets. He made a suggestion; we evaluated it and decided to pursue the plan by the time we reached the front door of school. We parted company; my colleague went to the office to sign up to use the little theater, and I went to our open-space classroom areas.

After the school's opening exercises, we took both home bases to the little theater for an archaeological dig. Small groups of four students rotated jobs like directing, dismantling the owl pellet, recording what was found, and drawing a picture of the items in situ. They glued the bones to brown paper to reconstruct as much as possible the skeletal remains of said mice. Things were labeled, and a working report was handed in. Who would have thought of using owl pellets to simulate an archaeological dig?

We tied things in with an audiovisual source I had used that presented the job of an archaeologist, and worked in biological information about owls, predatory birds, and the fate of their prey.

When Teams Are Larger, Agree on Themes

Scheduling may seem to work against thematic teaching; yet teachers can still follow themes if they are determined. In later years the administration created a core team of four to teach students across the three years of middle school. We had a team of four, but two of us were planning a three-year curriculum's scope and sequence plan. I would continue to teach social studies along with language arts at the sixth grade level, and the social studies department chairman would teach the social studies in grades seven and eight. What themes should we follow in seventh grade?

I wracked my brain for the major changes in our nation from the last half of the nineteenth century to the twentieth century, nearing its end at that time: the War between the States ended; western lands opened up with the railroad and the telegraph; immigrants came looking for a new life and jobs in the Industrial Revolution's aftermath that created huge cities; and of course the two world wars of the twentieth century in particular, as well as the Korean, Vietnam, and Cold Wars.

I came up with three themes: frontiers, immigration, and conflict. The social studies teacher put forth conflict and resolution, which worked. It was amazing: we had agreed on the themes for the seventh grade in about five or ten minutes. With the eighth grade curriculum, there was no argument from any quarter. The state of Virginia mandated covering the concepts of geography, government, and economics.

Later, when scheduling made it even more difficult for us to work in tandem, we could not combine classes to share programs and didn't plan shared activities. My colleague did read the students' term papers and research papers for their content, and at the end of the eighth grade, attended the debates on research paper topics that grew out of the social studies theme. We taught the seventh and eighth grade classes at different times; naturally students could not be in two places at once. But what went on in English was always linked to the social studies side of the shared theme.

As social studies marched through the state's requirements to ease the transition to high school, English students remained busy relating the two classes through planned activities. I felt that parallel teaching was quite successful. I will describe it in detail in chapter 8. This chapter just shows you the possibilities of working together, even if it is simply side by side.

Nothing Is Perfect

Alas, sometimes parallel teaching is rather isolated. You teach in your own classroom trusting that the colleague is sticking to the agreed upon theme or topics at roughly the same calendar period. You engage them in conversation to check now and then, but responses are short, even fuzzy, and you aren't quite sure how the correlation is working.

At that point, one has to have faith, if not in the plans or the parallel-teaching partner, then in the minds of the students. They will hear similarities in the two classrooms and make connections on their own. If they stop by after class to ask a question or seek clarification, you know something has worked at some level. That is a bit of proof, if not solid substantiation.

In Conclusion

In a later chapter, you'll hear about how we staged Ellis Island's immigration process in a large area with windows between two wings of the building. But until then, keep in mind that you don't have to do everything in an integrated way all the time from the very beginning.

Start with obvious connections in your own classroom; see which colleagues are teaching your students in subject areas that relate easily to yours. Tell them what you're doing, and ask when they teach such and such; or ask if they can give you some ideas of how to connect with their curriculum. Tell them what you had in mind as a possibility. Start lightly, start small, and allow for growth when you find opportunities or a kindred spirit with whom to cooperate.

INTEGRATING INTERDISCIPLINARY APPROACHES

Language before Content, or the Reverse?

With a little poetic license, I could say the early chapters advised, "Start slow, and go with the flow." *Slowly* is grammatically correct, but it doesn't rhyme. Starting slowly in integrating curriculum works to a degree and certainly gets thematic teaching going, if only down a short and narrow path. Take a content subject like social studies or science, and link it with reading. Some teachers go no further and accomplish a lot through the simple combination of fiction and fact.

Some researchers recommend integrating the four areas of language arts—reading, writing, listening, and speaking—before connecting with "broad areas of knowledge, such as social studies, mathematics, or ecology" (Lipson et al. 1993). A friend of mine in Colorado, who taught overseas as well as in the States, believes it is much easier to organize your lessons if you begin with a scientific principle or social studies concept, and then use literature, math, art, and music to support your theme. That worked best for me as well.

Interdisciplinary teaching can alternate between themes and topics with great ease. The problem comes in deciding which one is the horse and which one is the cart. Themes are abstractions. Topics are more like chapter titles in a book. My initial example of linking Greek myths in reading with a social studies chapter on ancient Greece is an example of a topic treated as a theme through correlation. The textbook chapter was titled "The Glory That Was Greece." Grecian glory is, indeed, a theme, but ancient Greece is a topic.

And there are other confusions that arise. Is economics a topic or a theme? It is probably a topic teachers could treat as a theme. That sounds like doublespeak. I would allow Plato's followers to discuss this thoroughly and philosophically, while we go on with the basics of planning theme/topic lessons. I say we can look at language skills as a bridge between the theme, or topic, and the learning experiences enlisted from other areas.

Prepare for Takeoff

In a way, when you have settled on the theme or topic you will investigate, then it all happens at once. Subject area teachers select information students will learn; language teachers decide how to involve communication skills, and choose materials that enhance the subject area text. Supporting teachers, like those in art and music, will suggest references and activities leading to possible projects directly involving students.

My Colorado colleague recommends planning with other teachers in a way that assigns responsibilities for the planning process. She says:

"Collaborate and plan with fellow grade-level teachers, as well. One year my first-grade team, all six of us, sat down and planned a six-week science unit for the purpose of giving at-risk children an opportunity to lead in the classroom, but it became my model for collaboration in any setting. Like a cooperative learning team, we each accepted a discrete role in the unit:

    a. web-based resource researcher,

    b. book-finder for independent reading or shared reading,

    c. science experiment planner,

    d. process evaluator (making sure we met standards, fulfilled our roles, reported to administration, etc.),

    e. process recorder—kept notes, questions, goals present in planning,

f. connections-finder to other subjects—art, math, music, etc."
(Szoka, "What I've Learned about Thematic Teaching,"
2008).

My friend actually enlists her primary grade students to help with planning, using K-W-L: What do I know? What do I want to know? What have I learned?

What happens if you are not a team of teachers working out a shared theme or topic across the disciplines of knowledge, meeting regularly, adapting grouping and scheduling to the activities planned, taking various responsibilities for the whole team to divide the labor and conquer all? Do not despair; it is possible to do theme teaching independently or through flexible planning sessions.

Team Planning Can Be Informal

Planning can be a team effort, but it can also be a short brainstorming or idea-sharing meeting, and then each teacher is on his or her own. Have short conferences while passing colleagues in the hall. Check with each other, when necessary, to see how everything is going. You are teaching the same students, so you will surely ask how they are doing in a colleague's class and share your view of a child informally or in a conference.

Laying out a chart is helpful. Some of that longer paper that is business letter width but goes on for about fourteen inches—we used to call it mimeograph paper—is useful here. Approach it horizontally, making the length the width for your purposes. Identify the theme or topic at the top. Then identify the areas of your subject that the curriculum requires you to address. Social studies teachers teach globe and map skills, timeline reading, time concepts, ethnic or national cultures, geography and biomes, and history.

English teachers should make columns for the language arts skills you need to cover regardless of theme (see appendix 1). I found I had five areas that I needed to include, one way or another: reading/literature, composition (writing), grammar, speech (oral skills), and library skills (finding sources, taking notes, making outlines, writing reports). At high school levels, library skills would be separated into using the library resources and doing research for reports, term papers perhaps.

Science teachers deal with assigned areas of weather, geology, energy, and such, which I believe change in emphasis according to the grade level.

To make it almost too simplistic, all you do now is keep the theme in mind, and ask yourself, "If the theme is (ancient Greece), what shall we read, what will we write about and in what form, what oral skills can we work on (small groups reporting findings?), what can we search out in the library, and how can I work grammar lessons into all of this?" When you plan your unit on library skills and written reports, consult your science or social studies colleagues for content topics. They can grade the same reports in terms of their curriculum requirements.

Check Local and Regional Resources

I remember learning of a school that kept a card file—a hard copy database—in the office. It held names of people who were good resources as speakers to visit the classroom, or to present an assembly program. They might be contact people at sites that welcome school groups, like historic battlefields, museums, parks, or industries. Organizations with educational interests like a chamber of commerce, a theater with children's programs, or agencies with a community-service focus would also be in the file.

Technology is changing our current society so fast that students may have two or three careers in their lifetimes and will certainly change jobs more than once. It seems that the era of a career in a single field seems to be ending as new opportunities are created almost daily. We must still make an effort to prepare students for the world of work, and not just higher academic challenges.

Bring in the World of Work

That opens us up to thinking of what people have to do *in the real world*. Budgetary constraints and mandated test demands may mean that vocational classes have been eliminated, but we can still do a lot. Classroom teachers can fill the void by at least exposing students to the real world, the world of daily work outside the home, by having them create basic products and projects they might do as employed adults. Employed adults need skills in constructing, drawing, advertising, speaking formally or just generally communicating, running a meeting, seeing a project through to completion, and doing research in labs or libraries.

Adults regularly produce television or video clips, maps, layouts, displays, journalism articles and columns, brochures, and performances in the arts: theater, music, graphic arts. They run computer programs, and some even create them. They do so independently, with someone else, or even in small working teams. Depending on the theme being used to integrate subject areas in schools, students may be involved in products and projects that cross the subject lines, and represent real adult experiences.

Themes for a Theme

"The five themes of geography provide a framework for teaching geography; they include location, place, human-environment interaction, movement, and region." So says one Internet entry for the National Council for Geographic Education (NCGE), referring to the work of a joint committee that produced the themes in 1984 (Keys-Mathews 1998). These themes were followed as a teaching framework until national standards were put forth ten years later.

When I inquired about their use from a teacher friend, I received this response via e-mail: "I used those five themes so much that even now, three years into retirement, I can cite them in my sleep: *location* (which can be either absolute or relative), *place* (not people; what makes this place 'this place'), *movement* (of people as well as ideas), *human-environmental interaction* (resources and how they are used), and *region* (things in common, e.g., the Middle East Region)" (Sciegaj 2008).

An English teacher in my middle school had attended a conference about the five geography themes and shared them with our sixth grade faculty, where language arts teachers also taught social studies. When your teaching assignment links the two subjects for you, the schedule usually provides back-to-back classes, essentially doubling the teaching time. The great benefit here is that you are preprogrammed to pick up one subject with the other. We used the geography themes to understand the regions of the world we were studying historically, but their usefulness did not stop there.

The geography themes turned up in English class (see figure 3.1), when we assigned fiction books for student reading. I always had a foreign

APPLYING THE FIVE THEMES OF GEOGRAPHY TO ADVENTURE FICTION AND BIOGRAPHY
Fill in the appropriate information for each theme as recognized in your book or novel. Quote any phrases copied from the text.
Indicate the page number on which the information is found.

		Page #
LOCATION: (Relative and Absolute)		
PLACE:		
REGION : (Biome)		
MOVEMENT:		
HUMAN and ENVIRONMENTAL INTERACTION:		

Figure 3.1. Five Themes of Geography

fiction book report assignment during one calendar month of the academic year. The geography theme *location* naturally dictated a summary paragraph or two describing the setting for the plot. Geographic locations for the story line would be enhanced by details about the particular place and the human activities taking place around the characters.

Plots never failed to describe how populations moved around—by foot, donkey or horseback, or powered transportation—and depending on the activities of the characters, the movement of goods and local products might be involved. The regional effects of the novel's setting usually explained the climate and resources available. Readers had to know what life was like for the characters and for any foreigners the plot dropped into their midst.

Classic examples of books to which the five themes of geography might be applied—because the books are *loaded* with information on region, flora and fauna, ethnic culture, habits and practices—are the Willard Price books, still in print in the United Kingdom through a division of Random House. Price traveled and wrote articles for the *National Geographic* during his career, and also wrote books about Hal and Roger Hunt, brothers, sons of a wild animal collector for zoos and circuses. Wikipedia has an article on Price with book summaries.

Seek out used copies of the Price books wherever you can find them. Every chapter is exciting enough for a Hollywood movie. They are the only books I used where a student insisted his mother buy a copy because he couldn't wait until the next school day to find out how the chapter's cliffhanger would be resolved. *African Adventure* is a good place to start in the multiple volume series, but you can go whaling or underwater diving, visit cannibals, sail down the Amazon River, and so forth in the other novels.

I am sure the social studies or geography instructor will be pleased with your supportive efforts if you teach English and assign books like these. Do not rely on receiving reinforcement automatically. Engage the students by asking how something in the novel relates to what they have been discussing with Mr. or Ms. So-and-so. Mention a particular idea yourself and ask students to offer others.

Readers who know my first book, *Brain-based Teaching for All Subjects: Patterns to Promote Learning*, will recall the discussion of the Culture Box in chapter 4. A culture box also works to support social studies concepts and help understand settings of novels. It represents, in a visual concept pattern, a model of any culture. Shown as six nested rectangles, it helps the brain's imaging system to visualize the six elements found wherever humans function on this earth: the individual *self*, the *family*, *educational options*, *religious practices*, *government types*, and *economic systems*.

What Ideas by What Means?

I am recalling a term my peers used, during our undergraduate days, for relatively unstructured or unorganized things, abstract and intangible: *loosey-goosey*. It is true that you can stumble onto good things, sources and ideas for interdisciplinary thematic teaching, just because a topic or theme is shared and the disciplines' content is established. It is a bit risky to rely on happy accidents to sustain your program, however. Sooner or later you should record on paper your best intentions for your students.

Two columns on a piece of paper, handwritten or in a word document, or on two sheets side by side, will do the trick. If you start out with pencil in hand, enter the plan into your computer when the thinking is complete. Ask yourself two questions:

- What ideas do I want the students to take away from this study?

- How will students learn these concepts?

Skills can guide you here. What should students actually do as they use information to produce something, becoming more involved? Are there appropriate projects or writing assignments, or presentations to the class that work here?

Note the resources needed: textbook assignments, other readings, visual aids like video and film that stream into classrooms via cables, direct location, websites or traditional computer programs if pertinent, speakers, and virtual or traditional field trips. Whether you storm your own brain or brainstorm with colleagues, keep organized records and samples of actual individual projects or class products.

Lipson et al. (1993) points out that integrated themes provide a valuable focus. Students understand what they are doing and why. The connections between subject areas allow the transfer of learning between contexts, and with brain research in mind, Lipson and coauthors point out that students acquire an integrated knowledge base more easily. Students may never forget what they have learned in this way. Those who integrate short-term into long-term knowledge are unlikely to forget what they have learned, and will transfer it to new situations more readily.

A Postscript from a Teacher of Primary Classes

"When my children asked, 'Are castles real?' we put together a unit on castles that included history, architecture, levers and cranes, geometry, art & music, literature, and even a virtual field trip. . . . It was a lot of fun. Another unit I did with first grade was 'Why is there air?' . . . and the outstanding activity was using blow-dryers to keep balloons and ping-pong balls in the air" (Szoka, e-mail, June 7, 2008).

SOCIAL STUDIES CAN RULE THE DAY: THEMES TO LESSON PLANS

A student studying societies as they developed across prehistory and recorded history, or even today's society, investigates a record of human living. Humans share abstractions. There are basic needs of food, shelter, and clothing dictating the earliest of economic systems. There are concerns for safety, which may have started with "the survival of the fittest," but certainly led to clans, tribes, and eventually rulers of some sort.

Passing on shared wisdom was an oral tradition for millennia, yielding folklore and folk literature as well. Humans yearn for beauty and developed folk art. Shared concern for each other led to valuing and conserving life, caring for each other, and making living places as attractive as possible. It might be argued that social studies is the source of all possible themes. It is certainly a unifying strand for any thematic curriculum. Even scientific discoveries occurred within developed societies across history. We can agree that, for these reasons, social studies rules the day when it comes to thematic teaching.

Theme or Topic?

Energy is a topic that can certainly be a unifying strand in combining subject areas. Treat this area of physics as a theme if you choose. Physics studies the energy of sound, light, motion, electricity, the atom, quarks, chaos theory, and more. Now we have the need for finding alternative energy sources because fossil fuel resources are being depleted, and our cavalier use of them is causing the ruination of the planet.

Human energy is a daily concern of most of the populace. A workforce needs energy to keep increasing production levels. Wellness, exercise, nutrition, sufficient rest—all these contribute to human energy levels about which we boast or complain of its lack. Health and physical education classes would certainly buy into a theme like energy. Music teachers would come on board, too. If energy can serve as a physics topic but also an integrating theme, other topics may have more possibilities than we may see at first. Science has many options for us, too.

So let us pick up our sledgehammer of the moment and ring the bell once again as we come up with social studies' related themes.

Linking Subject Areas

For more than a decade, my colleague and I had been correlating topics in science with language arts and social studies whenever possible: first in a team of four, then during several years of separate class schedules when we did share some of the same students. When teamed together with a group of forty-five to fifty students in two home bases, we decided to be more formally organized. Identified gifted students would continue the Cultures and Cuisines program of after-school cooking classes following the social studies sequence of world regions studied, but, during the school day, our team would work heterogeneously wherever possible.

For parents' open house night, we described our planned units as shared here. Be prepared for the old common noun for humanity, *man*. In 1984, we authors weren't savvy about using politically correct language. Old habits die hard, they say.

- Survival—The five units of interdisciplinary study present man's cycle of awareness, beginning with *Survival,* as he copes with nature and society, including the survival of a species and the survival of man himself as a separate biological being.

- Answers: Mythology and Astronomy—Having achieved a uniqueness in the animal kingdom, and having developed the skills to survive, man observed his surroundings more closely.

Out of this developed primitive and then more sophisticated religious and scientific understandings. These beginning observations of the natural world of man are pursued in a second unit involving *Answers: Mythology and Astronomy.*

- Scientific Law and Order—As man reaches still higher levels of sophistication in his analysis of what he sees in his environment, he begins to observe scientific laws: a study of famous scientists and an investigation of some of their chemical and physical experiments is made in the unit *Scientific Law and Order.*

- TV: Communicating through Energy—With these understandings of his world, man reaches out to communicate in wider and wider circles with fellow beings. A critique of television and a practical consideration of television programming is the subject of the unit *TV: Communicating through Energy.*

- Forces: Ecology and the Environment—The cycle of units is completed with a return to man's natural surroundings, as he learns to appreciate them in a more evaluative way. A study of animal fiction and environment is made in the unit *Forces: Ecology and Environment.* (Craig and Laster 1984)

What Do Students Get Out of This?

We really must have been selling the new curriculum that evening, because we had lists demonstrating how the integrated material would work toward classroom skills all students need:

Basic Skills	Thinking Skills	Research Skills
Reading for understanding, information, appreciation	Observing	Gathering data
	Classifying	Outlining
	Analyzing	Reporting, written/oral
Vocabulary building	Inferring	
Communication, written/oral	Predicting	Library skills: using the card catalogue,
	Hypothesizing	
Measuring	Interpreting	classifying books,
Computation		using varied sources
Problem solving		

We even included content objectives for language arts and science for each unit.

Objectives for the Survival Unit

The objectives for language arts class:

- To understand and appreciate the concept of personal survival in nature and some social settings.

- To develop a definition for the concept of survival.

- To investigate the personality traits of individuals who survive crisis situations in their lives, as portrayed in literature.

- To research the latest findings in brain studies to understand the reasons for man's continued survival as a biological being in an increasingly complex world.

The objectives for science class:

- To become familiar with the concepts of species survival and the use of the phrase "survival of the fittest."

- To consider human adaptations that separate man from other species.

- To understand the necessity of outdoor and personal survival skills, of just knowing your whereabouts.

- To be familiar with the human body systems as they evolved into modern man.

Scope and Sequence, an Overview

While preparing this manuscript, I resurrected my notes for this curriculum and found they were titled "Matrix/Grid of Curriculum." Down the left margin, we had listed the months of the school year, showing what would happen in science and for how long.

September and October

For example, in September and October, the *Survival* unit would be on the docket, and science classes would deal with orienteering—compass and map reading, maps themselves, and the physiology of the brain, source of our survival, along with fossils and forces of nature. There was an opportunity for a wonderful field trip, too.

For a few years, back in the 1970s, there had been a billboard for the Thunderbird Museum of Early Man, about forty minutes south down the interstate highway. World War II "ducks" took students from one side of the Shenandoah River to the other and back, through the shallows and bottom fields where a farmer had found spearheads. We saw ongoing archaeological excavations, and the marshy area where prehistoric animals were driven to be bogged down and more easily killed. And there was a small museum, all nearby. What we learned, we took back to class (see figure 4.1).

In language arts, literature, research, and writing would be involved. Students would read survival literature, do some writing in the first person, *find* an uncharted island—describing and mapping it, and use findings in brain research to decide whether archaeologists use the right hemisphere processes or the left. The social studies basis for these activities was map skills and a study of early man. We would now call that a study of early humans.

	GOAL	STEP 1	STEP 2	STEP 3	STEP 4	STEP 5
T A S K	Clan Record for Survival	Draw and label the parts of a tool your clan could use. Write the directions for making it.	Draw and label the parts of the technology for roasting hunted and killed game. Write directions for using it. List the game you could roast.	Make a list of the materials the men of the clan should look for to make tools and weapons.	Make a list ("shopping list") of foods the clan women should gather.	Glue steps 1-4 on a poster sheet. Letter the clan's name and put a clan symbol by it. List your names in the bottom corner.

Figure 4.1. Procedure Frame for a Clan Record

November and December

During November and December, and sliding into January, our notes show the second unit, *Answers: Mythology and Astronomy*, taking over. Science class focused on astronomy, constellations, space, the solar system, matter, atoms, and chemistry. But as social studies left the Middle East, archaeology, Mesopotamia, and Egypt, it moved to Greece and Rome. Language arts made the adjustment.

Language arts shifted to looking at the survival of civilization in superstitions and mythology, researching Greek mythological characters that the science teacher linked to the zodiac constellations and the popular horoscopes that some still follow. Eventually we read Roman myths and created a Roman newspaper. It was a newspaper the Romans would have read had the Romans published one. If you consider doing this project, it is probably wise to focus on the culture of the Republic rather than the Empire. That way you control the scope and content for your students.

Producing newspapers is a project that pays many dividends. Students work singly, but more often together in pairs or groups. If time is limited, a newspaper can be a whole-class project. It isn't as difficult as it was in the middle of the last century when the teacher typed every child's article in two-and-a-half-inch columns onto what was affectionately known as a *ditto*. Turning the crank of the ditto machine produced those purple-ink copies, fresh off the cylinder, and only needing to be stapled in one corner.

Another process was to type the columns, cut them out, glue them to a backing, and make master copies of each three-columned page to photocopy en masse. Now computers give you a choice of two- and three-column page layouts in word processing programs, but even easier to use are the computer programs for setting up newspapers. Familiar old names of such programs included Print Shop and Newsroom. You may know what is available today. Teachers' websites, publications, and teachers' stores selling all sorts of classroom materials will have them.

Do get class sets of editions from the local newspaper, or bring in copies you have saved from your subscription. Just clipping representative articles will do. It is really nice if a newspaper journalist is willing to come and speak to your class, but just having students look at, read, and pull apart what is obvious about news articles can be sufficient. And then supply them with a visible reminder of a news article, before they write one.

In the concept pattern shown in figure 4.2, an oval and an inverted triangle are placed in the rectangle representing the headline. The oval is a noun symbol, and the inverted triangle represents the verb. A retired newspaper writer spoke to a summer workshop for middle school students and told us headlines always have a subject and a verb. I consistently used parts of speech symbols in grammar lessons (Laster 2008), hence their appearance in this concept model.

Scheduling is not a perfect science, and teachers must remain flexible. Even if you plan so that classes can coordinate, groups may not stay together on the topic, certainly not always on a daily basis. Then too, teachers cannot be absolutely positive of how long a particular class group will take to absorb a topic or understand a process.

Our jottings show that science classes maintained a two months per unit pace until March, when only one month was devoted to electronics, television, and videotaping a news program. Back in December, I was already easing into the Middle Ages in social studies, which meant reading historical fiction in language arts, role-playing, and writing first-person narratives as an individual living on a manor during the Middle Ages: "A Day in the Life of . . ." But by January, we were studying the Renaissance. That was the rebirth period, you recall.

January and February

The unit was *Scientific Law and Order*. Chemistry, electricity, and energy ruled the discussions in science class. The Renaissance moved reading for language arts into the area of scientists' biographies and library reports on inventors. As March approached, Britain's Industrial Revolution described huge changes in people's lives. British mystery writers enjoy worldwide reputations; we read Agatha Christie titles, and discussed genre and author style.

March

In late February and early March, social studies kept marching onward with the political revolution in France, the world wars with Germany, and the ideological revolution in Russia. It was the perfect time to arrive at the fourth unit, *TV: Communicating through Energy*. In science students learned how television actually telecast programs and prepared to tape a

News Article

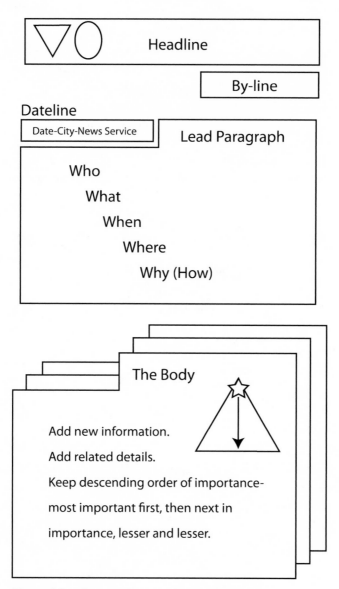

Figure 4.2. Concept Pattern for News Articles

school news program. In English we began a study of television and its effects as studied by sociologists and psychologists. A set of library filmstrips reported on children's behavior after watching violence on television, for example. Social studies shifted to Asia, almost without our notice.

April and May

April and May brought us around to the fifth and final unit, *Forces: Ecology and Environment.* We were traveling through Asia and Africa in the last of the social studies textbook sections. Animal fiction was a natural reading choice, and one of the reading series books had an article on how Henry David Thoreau, an early environmentalist, lived for two years in the woods of New England. While science classes involved ecology and biomes, language arts added folktales, and students wrote and bound original books.

Survival: The First Unit

A Variety of Reading Choices

Back when the year started and sixth graders were in the middle school as the new kids on the block, they were nervous, and it was a good time to read aloud *My Side of the Mountain* by Jean Craighead George (1959), about a New York City boy who runs away from home and survives in the woods of New York State. With the Survival unit, small groups read these books:

- J. C. George's *Julie of the Wolves.* New York: Harper, 1972.

- Armstrong Sperry's *Call It Courage.* New York: Scholastic, 1940.

- Scott O'Dell's *Island of the Blue Dolphins.* New York: Dell Publishing Group, 1960.

- Robb White's *Deathwatch.* New York: Dell Publishing, 1972.

- Anne Frank's *The Diary of a Young Girl.* New York: Pocket Books, 1953.

- Gloria Skurzynski's *Lost in the Devil's Desert.* New York: Wm. Morrow and Company, 1992.

Your friendly librarian will be happy to help you find survival adventure books for readers at younger and older ages than middle school. There is no dearth of possibilities.

Always check the adopted reading series in your school system. They plan collections that include nonfiction articles, poetry, and all genres of literature. We found wonderful articles on lemmings (from *Reader's Digest* for August 1970) and the armadillo (from *National Wildlife* for December/January 1972) in our reading series. A perfect fit was the excerpt from a book called *Carlos Charles* by Patrick and Shirley Murphy, dealing with an airplane wreck in the Central American jungle.

A story called "Cave of Danger" in the reader *Serendipity* (Houghton-Mifflin, 1975), demonstrated the need for rules for survival in a spelunking situation, and also the character traits of a survivor in a dangerous situation. Don't forget such classics as Daniel Defoe's *Robinson Crusoe*, and Johann David Wyss's *Swiss Family Robinson*. Reading books for upper grades often have articles on human and animal survival in natural surroundings, and also the survival of folk wisdom, superstitions, and ideas in societies as times and technologies change. Lower grade readers have stories and articles on animals, wild animals, and pets.

National Geographic magazine provides a wealth of articles on the conditions in wilderness areas and surviving in them. If you leave them lying casually but tastefully on a display table, students will pick them up for the cover picture and glance inside. Sometimes perusing the photos and reading the captions are enough to get students' minds interested in something new, which could lead to further reading and exploration on their part.

In and Out of the Classroom

You will read later about the cave paintings on the classroom divider screen, but another bulletin board display consisted of "Ten Commandments for Survival" as lettered on gray construction paper, imitating the stone tablets God gave to Moses in the Bible story. In this same vein, a personal essay on what expectations students had before coming to middle school asked them to suggest the skills they found they needed to cope with this big transition. While the idea of the survival theme is inherent here, any transition represents a personal frontier, a theme discussed in chapter 7.

In general, classroom lesson activities were quite varied. You already know about sanitized owl pellets and their archaeological potential. I had introduced the concept of maps, and different types of maps (Laster 2008, chap. 4); the uncharted island activity was related to that. Students imagined being stranded on an uncharted island, and they wrote the story of how they arrived there, where they were, and how they would survive. They were to refer to latitude and longitude readings, and appropriate climate and geographical information. They made a detailed map with its basic parts.

In science class, students mapped their way to school from their homes, learned about azimuths and how to read a conventional compass once they had established where north was, and navigated a six-point orienteering course on the school campus. Small groups studied selected body systems and reported to the class using appropriate visual materials.

A local church had a retreat center located in a rural area, and one year we had an overnight field trip there. We cooked our own food, watched the constellations through a large telescope, played memory games, and took a survival test about an imaginary situation, which we discussed afterward. In the morning, we followed marked orienteering trails before returning to school after lunch.

Another year we used the facilities of the local park across the street from our school. We had Cave Man Day in the Park. My colleague set up orienteering markers for several trails ahead of time so the groups could be locating their color-coded trails at the same time. A retired Boy Scout leader came to show us how early humans must have started fires with flint and one of those sharpened sticks twirled into tinder with a small bow. Once the fire was going, the student clans (small groups) took ten-minute stints turning a chicken on the spit over the fire. Meanwhile a local librarian was telling about the two years he had lived with Indians in Central Virginia.

When the chicken was cooked, I had the privilege of carving it with a prehistoric knife—most impressive—just think of a small, but quite sharp, arrowhead. Everyone sampled the chicken. We also went around the area picking natural materials to take back to school. We were going to paint cave walls with what we found, such as crushed grass and bush berries. Flattened and torn brown grocery bags served nicely for cave walls. Overlapped on a screen divider, around a buffalo painted cave-style on brown paper, they looked quite realistic and definitely prehistoric. And these activities were selected from only the first unit theme.

Seeing Stars: The Second Unit

The second unit with mythology and astronomy involved more content correlation than shared activities. My science/math teacher colleague used a space simulation involving a space society (*Galaxy*, Interact of California, 1980). Students learned to take samples to estimate a total, using corn grains, spoons, and cups, and projecting the number of students in school, books in the library, and eventually the stars in the sky.

Students researched elements in the solar system, constellations in the night sky, read sky charts, selected a group of stars to create a new constellation and wrote its story as well as designating the star magnitudes, represented by colors. They researched the planets and created a table on the dividing screen between the class areas to compare size, distance from the sun, orbiting moons, size of orbits, and such discovered information.

In language arts class, mythology held sway via reading book selections and individual myths, read and viewed with the current technology. They created name acrostics for the gods and goddesses and heroes by arranging large, colorful letters spelling the mythological character's name down the middle of the paper. Then they wrote the character's story through the letters so that the letter fit into the word crossing it.

This was a time for reading excerpts from the myth-epic about the Trojan Horse, excerpts from Homer's *Odyssey*, the journeys of Ulysses, about the excavations of Troy by Heinrich Schliemann, and for writing original myths to explain natural phenomena. Graph paper made illustrating mosaics fairly uncomplicated. The excavations at Pompeii showed how the Romans adopted the Greek pantheon, and *Detectives in Togas* (Winterfeld 1956) gave us a taste of everyday Roman life.

As mentioned in the Scope and Sequence section, a computer program for young students, Newsroom, made creating a newspaper easy. If the Romans had had newspapers, what would they have been like? We had the students produce one. The Newsroom program has been updated, and today's classes might consider publishing their news articles as blogs, or on a class website.

Scientific Law and Order: The Third Unit

The company that produced *Galaxy*, Interact of California, had another tempting tidbit in the catalogue, which turned out to be a winner. The Interact simulation was already worked out from start to finish.

We removed the divider screen between our room areas, using the combined classroom areas to arrange desks showing, visually as well as spatially, the pyramid structure of medieval society. Small groups of serfs planned crop plantings and decided on field use—some fields had to lie fallow to recover from repeated harvests. They sat in small groups at one end of the open area. Stewards had their desks nearby, but not too near. A roll of the dice determined the weather and crop results for the year. In a fair year or foul, a portion of the crops went to pay taxes.

There were a few knights and nobles as you moved away from the serfs, and we did have a lord and lady, if not a royal couple. There were two bishops, representing the strength of the church, off to one side of the upper ranks of society. Students loved role-playing the time period. Regular journal writing, grammar, and spelling were maintained during the simulation's time frame.

The Awakening of the Renaissance

In social studies we also learned that the Crusaders brought back scrolls, books from the Holy Land in which the wisdom of the Greeks and Romans had been preserved by the Arab and Persian scholars after the fall of Rome and the burning of the great library in Alexandria, Egypt. Science classes had already enacted roles in a space academy via the *Galaxy* simulation game. Mythology and constellations were left to the heavens; famous astronomers like Copernicus and Galileo joined scientists and inventors.

Our librarians culled biographies of scientists for our students. To get a grasp of time in terms of centuries, students who had made personal timelines earlier in the year made one for a scientist's life based on the reading of his or her biographies and additional research. Science classes used the biography reading as a springboard for several activities: researching an inventor's field, designing an experiment to illustrate the person's lifework, and giving a short biographical sketch to the class. Following the active learning trend, each student taught the science class, providing materials for each member of the class to do the experiment.

In language arts, students decided on three adjectives best describing the character traits of the scientist in their biographies. Using the term *adjective* was a subtle reminder of grammar while focusing on a theme-related reading assignment. When a graphic organizer was used, four adjectives were chosen. The inventor's name was in a center box; the adjectives labeling the personality traits were written in connecting areas leading to four frames representing the inventor's actions that demonstrated these traits. There is a website for graphic organizers where you can download your choices and where you will find this organizer for analyzing characters.

After posting their vertical timelines, the students presented oral reports wearing representative costumes and stating everything in the first person to portray the subject of their biographies. They also created ten puns based on their inventor's career. Example: "One thing you can say about my job: it doesn't 'bug' me" (entomologist).

Again, the reading series used in our school system supported the themed unit with articles and short biographies, including one on Leonardo da Vinci. Interact of California published *Reading Contracts* for individual projects focused on four areas in each packet. We used a helpful list of inventors in the first packet, which included biography/autobiography contracts, still available today.

TV—Communicating through Energy: The Fourth Unit

In language arts class we set out to consider the place of television in society as a whole, and in students' personal lives, to be aware of the criticism directed at television programming and its societal effects, and to simulate roles of sociologists and statisticians to prepare reports on findings. Students worked with program schedules from three commercial channels and a PBS channel. They also kept a record of what they watched on TV during a single week. We devised a color-coding system to determine the amount of time allotted to program types at the time. Percentages were calculated based on total hours of airtime for a week per program category.

Students surveyed people in various age groups to collect data on typical viewing habits.

The findings resulted in some intriguing graphs and other statistics under the headings "TV and Society" and "TV and the Individual." The graphic material was displayed on classroom bulletin boards along with print media references to television from current articles, cartoons, and comic strips.

While in science class, students learned how programs were actually telecast, and they prepared to produce and tape a school news program. They would investigate other methods of communication, find elements that compose a career in communication, learn to budget time and work cooperatively, and produce a television show. Fortunately there were sources like "A Day in the Life of . . . a television reporter," which worked as a good introduction to the whole idea. The school news program involved conducting interviews, writing, designing graphics, creating a studio set, and finding unusual locations in school to do after-school taping with the portable camcorder.

One year we visited a TV station. The students had watched the credits on a taped news program and selected a job they might want to do. They researched the job, wrote a description, shared it with the class, and eventually wrote letters to those people at the television station. One recipient answered and invited us to visit the TV station. We accepted with enthusiasm.

The field trip to Channel 4 (in Washington, DC) included touring the studio first before watching a telecast. Students with specific interests got to stand near and observe, for example, a cameraman during the news broadcast. We found out that the anchors, who remain seated throughout the program, are appropriately dressed from the waist up, but may have shorts or blue jeans on below the table level. Why completely change clothes when only half of you is actually seen?

The group received weather booklets from the meteorologist. Audiences at home may not know he is really watching the wall-screen monitor as he gestures toward the TV screen's map with the isobars and moving storm fronts that viewers see. And of course, when we returned home, we wrote thank you notes to the newsroom people and technology support team.

Once back in our hometown, the students dived into their own school news production teams, interviewing people for planned stories, writing news and sports reports, and planning commercials for the school store. The actual television taping was done after school with the large portable video camera of that time, using the cleared hallways and the open area of the little theater with its thrust stage as the main studio. Oh, what they learned. . . .

As a *culminating activity*, we watched ourselves on a television set, and the finished school news program was shared with parents along with the displays of projects and reports.

But we had our fifth and last theme-unit of the year still to go. Today's students can easily make copies of their broadcast on DVDs as a record of their participation in this memorable project.

Forces—Ecology and Environment: The Fifth Unit

You can imagine what our objectives were for this one, as the topic is front and center in our lives now in the twenty-first century as it had not been in the last century. Language arts jump-started the unit when I read aloud the Willard Price book *Safari Adventure* about poachers on a wild animal preserve in Kenya.

We interacted, again, with Interact of California, using their simulation called *Ecopolis*. It re-created the environmental shifts across one hundred and fifty years' history of an area in the United States as the population changed. The simulation had an activity where students answered a questionnaire on ecology problems at the beginning and end of the unit to see if their attitudes had changed. Students became acquainted with Henry David Thoreau's *Walden* when small groups tackled selected chapters. Other science simulations exist today.

Science classes even delved into population growth by exercising math skills to calculate the geometric increase in a population of rabbits at the end of one, two, and three years, if the rabbit population typically doubled each successive month. One can imagine students applying the idea of the size of rabbit families to their own experiences with siblings, making a human connection.

Language arts classes headed to the library to research biomes and write reports on indigenous animals. They read animal fiction, illustrating a scene in a shoebox made into a peep-box. They wrote poems and original stories, and played the game *wari* (the original African name for the Indonesian game *mancala*). The art teacher helped students make African animal masks with brown paper, glue, markers, and staples. The storeroom held an old reading series with a wealth of sources in addition to our current set of readers. Just imagine the African folktales like the one about the talking yam.

This chapter has to stop somewhere, and the end of an academic year when science and language arts were wedded to social studies is a perfect place. Know that we had many other related activities that I did not encapsulate for you in these pages. I didn't mention any films, videos, slides, and the lowly filmstrips of the twentieth-century classrooms, or all of the other possible resources today. But we did use those available to us. I do hope you sensed how much energy and enthusiasm there was for students immersed in these themes, living the aspects of experience that they provided.

Best of all, I looked forward to going to school each day.

THEME-BASED LEARNING ACTIVITIES

More Involvement, More Learning

From where you sit in the ballpark, your sight line might be good, bad, or even excellent. From where you sit in the classroom of your childhood memory, a few favorite school assignments may still stand out in your mind, accompanied by some degree of pleasure.

We don't usually hold in our memories the best test we ever took, though we might remember an earned grade or two. Very few textbook chapters are going to dominate our pleasant recollections of classroom learning unless they had some gory illustrations. Most everyone can name a so-called favorite teacher or two, or three, but usually for the way they taught, for the learning atmosphere they created, for the way they appreciated you as a student. Graduates remember ". . . what we did in Miss Thomas's room."

If We Learn by Doing, What Should We Be Doing?

Most elementary students love making things, and drawing pictures. They look forward to getting to the next grade level when they can do some neat project an older sibling or friend had done. They might have been inspired by exhibits at a learning fair. They have seen what has been going on in classrooms where they delivered a note for the teacher or visited for another reason. Class projects in hallway display cases catch their attention as items change with the seasons. As visitors walk by a classroom with projects on display, they think, "There's a lot going on in that room." Projects can come from home, or class work in small groups.

From a teacher's perspective, projects can be appealing, especially if they are completed in time for a school's open house or parents' night. More can result, though, than just admiring glances. When students stand near their projects to answer questions, they feel important and knowledgeable; they develop a sense of pride in their work. Displays do decorate the room, but they also give a chance for students to compare, and develop taste and evaluative skills. Work habits can be instilled, standards of quality nurtured, respect for ideas, creativity, and craftsmanship developed via projects.

Some students are last-minute producers, and some are reluctant to make an attempt, lest they not live up to their own expectations. Few students can hold out individually when classmates are enthusiastically talking about an idea on which they are working and how it is coming along. The unproductive student will feel pressed to bring in something, and may learn, albeit the hard way, about planning ahead, organizing, time management, and quality.

Parents enjoy seeing their children interested in producing something, and often take part in supporting the project. Cynicism suggests that occasionally, the night before the due date, there is a crisis moment requiring a trip to the store. Parents, who genuinely want to help their child without taking over the project and making it their job, share the moments of learning remembered fondly years later. I have drafting tools from when my father helped me make neat, block letters on a Pearl Harbor poster project in fourth grade. I'm part of history.

Brains Like Projects Too

Why assign projects? Some teachers may see projects as a way to keep students interested. Let them do something they like. Here the theory of multiple intelligences (Gardner 1983) overlaps with the idea of learning styles, preferred ways of learning: aurally, kinesthetically, verbally, visually. Projects have the benefit of involving several senses and mental processes at once. Perhaps the brain likes to be more involved than just being in a lecture, listening and trying to connect ideas.

Projects are a means of communication. The student has to decide what information is necessary to put forth and possibly why. In thinking through how the message should be expressed, the student clarifies the material in his or her own mind, and then considers the format in which to present the information best. The more consideration that occurs, the more sifting, reviewing, evaluating, and selecting the student must do. Repeated processing of information creates better understanding and mental storage.

In considering projects as a teaching tool, but also as a form of communication, teachers can give students personal choices. Think about choosing a project as selecting the right means of delivering the message. Students appreciate having choices because they feel more in control of their learning, more involved. Depending upon the age of the students, choices may be open—almost anything goes—but it is wiser to limit them. Some students can never make up their minds when no limits exist.

Think of helping a toddler learn to make choices by choosing the clothes to wear one morning. Chaos and frustration can result from opening the closet door and cheerfully asking, "What do you want to wear today?" Most child development experts suggest asking, "Do you want to wear your red outfit or the blue one?" Besides, you are teaching the color words, too. With school-age students, limiting choices focuses more on teaching aims. Teachers can use the communication principle as a filter to better tailor projects to their own goals as well.

Using Information for What Purpose?

Usually teachers assign projects to have students use information they want them to learn and remember. The students are forced to focus on it in analytical ways, manipulating and reworking it to transfer the message in an appropriate form. Teachers can concern themselves with general areas of idea sharing: oral presentations, construction projects as models, or those involving graphic art techniques. Other projects may result in various writing products, research, or even computer programs with older students.

And while teachers inevitably evaluate results and assign grades, checking for quality—neatness, spelling, appearance, appeal, clarity, accuracy—they can also help students organize their assignments, break the tasks into steps, estimate time required, and suggest ways to check work before handing it in. You have seen the procedure frame for a clan project in figure 4.1. We will look into procedure frames that help with assignment tasks later. The question remains, how best can this information be delivered?

There is another value inherent in the project method. No matter what students are assigned or encouraged to do, the skills they use and the products that result immerse them, not just incidentally, in real-life experiences. They are creating results that adults in the workforce repeat each day as part of their jobs. A curriculum that allows students to explore skills and crafts leading to finished projects not only introduces them to those activities, but lets them see wider opportunities where they might find their personal talents and interests.

Project Panorama

I would like to share a list of projects—a mind-dump. When you brainstorm with your own brain, I call it a *mind-dump*. I took the alphabet approach to see what my memory would resurrect as to projects and activities for each letter. Later, as I went through my files preparing to write this book, I found *An ABC of Student Projects* from Don Treffinger (Treffinger and McEwen 1989). My copy dated from 1981, but when I contacted him, Dr. Treffinger shared a copyrighted version from 1988. You will find a copy of his alphabet list of projects in appendix 2.

The ABCs of Possible Projects: Get Them Involved

A architectural schematics: elevations, mock blueprints, cross sections, floor plans; aquariums, ant farms, alphabet lists like this one on projects

B "bibles" on various topics, biographies, original books, booklets, brochures, bulletin boards, "small businesses"

C calendars, campaigns, catalogues, city planning, collages, comics, comparative studies, cooking projects, creative writing: "A Day in the Life of . . . ," cross sections

D diagrams (labeled), dialogues, diaries, dioramas, displays, dramas (skits, musicals, plays)

E   election campaigns, examples, experiments

F   fabulous facts (statements), fantasies: "What if . . .?"

G   original games, graphs, group work (small)

H   handwork, historic fiction, how-to projects

I   investigations

J   journalism approaches

K   kaleidoscopes, kits, kilns for pottery

L   learning centers, letters in *persona* correspondence files: invitations, thank you notes, personal and business letters

M   magazines, maps (picture, special topic), memory devices, miniature museums, models, movies, murals, music, musicals

N   newspaper mock-ups and separate features

O   outlines, overviews, operas, operettas

P   paintings, pamphlets, panels, plantings, plays, poetry, political cartoons, posters, puppet shows, puzzles

Q   questions and answers, quiz shows

R   radio programs, read-aloud sharing, research, research papers

S   shoeboxes for parade-float bases, shoeboxes with eyeholes and light openings for peep-box scenes, sketches, skits, surveys

T   team competitions, TV ads, television shows (news, talk-show formats), travelogues, term papers, terrariums, use "think-pair-share" to produce something, timelines, tombstones, and Ten Commandments

U   underground images/visuals (2-D and labeled)

V   videos, visuals

W   walking tours, writing of all kinds: essays, reports, rhymes, poems, stories [aim at different ages of readers/audiences]

X   "X-rays"

Y   years in history (overviews) in various formats

Z   zoos: cages, creatures, and habitats

At this point, you might stop and make your own alphabetical mind-dump from projects you have either already created yourself as a student, or remember doing with a class during your teaching career. Hard copy or computer generated, a list is a record of opportunities to which you can continually add more ideas for the proverbial rainy day.

What to Read about the Theme

This is the moment when some people would use the term *problematic*. Reading can be an end in itself; it also leads to other areas of language like writing and speaking. It is difficult to treat it separately without creating a type of mental octopus that leads one's train of thought astray.

Reading can result in projects of all sorts and types as the readers report to the teacher or the rest of the class, individually or in groups. Reading and writing skills can be combined to produce a research project, or to use information in creative form such as historic fiction, science fiction, skits and plays, or poetry. Literature groups have been used to good effect at all grade levels. Four or five students read the same novel, discuss it with differing amounts of guidance, and share the results with the rest of the class in different ways.

Sometimes we teachers are a bit nervous about relinquishing our position of adult leader, or as one supervisor quoted, "Fount of all wisdom, the 'sage on the stage.'" We worry that we will lose control of the orderly process of learning, and students will just socialize and not take their responsibility seriously. I must remind readers of the brain research finding about the importance of a social setting to learning. It works, and it can be efficient, as well as involving more students sharing in the same amount of class time.

Provide structure for the literature groups with a time limit and an immediate goal to accomplish. It might be in the form of a memo with a checklist or a procedure frame with the full goal described in steps (seen in chapter 4). Then step back and allow enough time for the group to accomplish one or two steps that day. But don't walk away; walk around. Amble slowly, stopping to rest on the edge of your desk or at a bookshelf, near enough to listen without being so close that students feel on edge because you might overhear or even interrupt them. If you are needed, someone will raise a hand and ask you to come over to answer a question.

At this point, other forms of projects can be employed for the sharing. A bulletin board display can be the result if each group compiles a representative illustration for the main events of the important chapters. The illustrations can be posted consecutively, like a comic strip, adding captions beneath each chapter's scene, with the book's author and title in a frame at the beginning, somewhat like a book cover.

With five groups, five plot analyses, and a genre-naming title for the bulletin board, you have a large area of wall space decorated with something students can study if their minds wander from the lesson. Some may be tempted to read the other books. Others may notice the different artistic techniques in the colored drawings. Still others will remember how their particular groups discussed the book and wonder about how the resulting pictorial version stacks up against the competition. You've stirred up a lot of thought.

Books Have a Lot of Competition These Days

Individual reading assignments that we've called book reports for generations take some ingenuity in planning these days. Students have experiences with video games, computer games, and DVDs of films, not to consign to the sideline television options that have made people born since 1946 all part of the television generation. Books play second or third fiddle.

Marie Winn (1978) points out that between 1948 and 1950 the number of television sets in homes went from a few thousand to fifteen million (p. 99). The effect of appealing programming right in the living room meant sets were turned on from early morning children's shows to the late night news. Formerly, homes had had radios playing all during the day; now they sometimes treated television the same way: it even played to empty rooms.

At first librarians thought television fostered reading as youngsters came looking for *Lassie*, Albert Payson Terhune's beloved dog story that inspired the American television series. Half a century later, we know the truth, and if we have kept up with the times, we teachers have adjusted to painful reality and use assignment methods to assure that our students actually read curriculum-related books. We can monitor their choices too.

Back to the Main Message

My librarian cohorts would pull books from the collection, selecting those that fit the theme of the moment. Usually they asked me to look over the lot, which numbered four or five more than the number of students in the class after I might have rejected a couple. You didn't want the last student stuck with the leftovers; everyone needs to have options, even the last student—the caboose on the train—for whatever reason. Motivation is often a factor; busy schedules complicate too. Let us not judge student character here.

The librarians set the books aside on a library table where my students could find them. Since the novels were for middle school students, I wanted at least 100 or 110 pages of reading. The library kept a list on file, which sped up the process when we studied the theme the next school year. They even made multiple copies of the list so students could take one. I kept copies in my files too. Had I made my own copies, they would have been files on my computer in a *theme-reading* folder. In elementary schools, a class set of selected books could be checked out and taken to the classroom.

In literature groups, there is peer pressure to read the book. In individual assignments, the pressure is different, and it helps to structure the reading for the final reckoning. My students read a book every month and sometimes two per six-week grading period. I usually provided something called a procedure frame (see figure 5.1), a version of cognitive psychologists' term for the boxes that frame the parts of a generalized experience, like visiting a museum or going to the movies. I described it for them as an empty comic strip.

In a procedure frame, a smaller box begins a series of boxes and announces the goal and task. The remaining boxes break the task into sequential steps where the directions are given. The left-to-right order eliminates the impression that an item at the top of the list is the most important. Students view it as a calendar, inferring time as well as process. It makes evaluation efficient for both student and teacher.

The true-life adventure assignment was used in a geography theme, but would fit a survival theme as well, and could be logically related to a frontier theme too. It's a matter of making the connections, a rationale that is clear to the students when you introduce the type of book. Themes lend themselves beautifully to biographies and autobiographies for reading assignments. Today's students face a changing future with overwhelming options and possibilities. What better way to exemplify lives well lived to a generation whose main goal is to be successful than to let them read about those who did just that, but not always with wealth in mind?

GOAL	STEP 1	STEP 2	STEP 3	STEP 4
To respond to a "true-life" adventure.	Abstract from the book you read, the features and characteristics of the geographical setting.	Read through the book again by skimming through important chapters. (Refer to the novel pattern in your pattern books to help analyze the book's plot.) Select an excerpt to read aloud to the class.	Be prepared to tell the audience how the setting determined the outcome of the person's adventure. This should take no more than one other minute.	Write no more than one side of a page in cursive, unless you use a word processor or type; describe the personality of the person who lived this adventure. If a group was involved in the event, pick one person who seemed to manage better than the others in the circumstance and describe his/her character or personality. Support your statements
	Create a poem to express this description of the setting. Allude to or suggest the possibilities of such a location for living things, and especially humans.	Aim for 2-3 minutes. Don't go over four. Practice to read it with realistic expression and appropriate phrasing.		Read out loud (don't cheat) what you've written to be sure the meaning is clear, and your ideas haven't been sabotaged by your spelling, punctuation, or sentence structure.
	Underline title on top line, center author's name beneath, and # of pages in text beneath that.	Pacing is important, and eye-contact with the audience helps.		Copy neatly to hand in.

T
A
S
K

Figure 5.1.   Procedure Frame for a True-Life Adventure Novel

Famous people's lives included missteps, misadventures, and possibly poor judgment, not consistently stupendous accomplishments. Through failures and occasional rewards, their persistence, and having the best intentions for all, led to success, both in peer approval and material success. They achieved fame *and* fortune. Their contributions to their contemporary societies were handed on to the future. As Sir Isaac Newton (1642–1727) asserted in his letter to Robert Hooke (February 5, 1675), "If I have seen further, it is by standing on the shoulders of giants." We don't have to preach to youngsters; they will get the message from historical and contemporary role models.

Sometimes we teachers serve up an hors d'oeuvre buffet. We choose class time readings to discuss, or assign, excerpts from classics and contemporary books, knowing students may never read the whole book—it's the exposure principle again—but some may be hooked. One delicious taste, and they will seek out the whole book for themselves.

No matter their age, read aloud to your students. Some books are a large mouthful to swallow—I'm thinking of *The Jungle* by Upton Sinclair—but they make a point about your theme that students should not miss. Reading to them will get the point across. You model oral reading skills, get their interest, and they hear what they, themselves, may never choose to see on the printed page. Sinclair's novel made quite a stir over the slaughterhouse situation in the first decade of the last century, but what school student would seek out a description of hard labor, blood, and gore on their own? It's economics from several standpoints.

The final product of many a novel reading is an essay, of course. But constructions like peep-boxes, shoebox-based parade floats for reading month, dioramas, or marketing posters can vary the report form. Instead of asking for a formal character analysis, why not suggest that students think of topics that their book's main character might want to discuss with a psychologist or a counselor? Think of the troubled Hamlet, or Holden Caulfield of teenage angst fame (*The Catcher in the Rye*, by J. D. Salinger) sharing their unsettling thoughts.

Teachers can get a lot of mileage out of the required literature series. Of course this represents the read-and-discuss tradition, but why abandon a worthwhile tradition? Look how many book groups meet in every town and city in the nation in the twenty-first century. People who love to read love to talk about the ideas and the effects of an author's efforts. With several series from which to choose, I never ran out of sources. We read, discussed, analyzed, and developed vocabulary all under the umbrella of the moment.

Develop a Concept through Theme Readings

It is part of the job of an English teacher to teach the concept of the essay. Young students see parents reading the newspaper in hand or online. They understand writing reports on different topics. Some aspire to journalism. As students move through school, concepts develop with their various dimensions. Primary students may learn the concept of a paragraph, but finally, they see that putting together a number of paragraphs creates a full report or essay.

It has always intrigued me how, once I have a topic in mind, I see evidence of it wherever I look. The mind is sensitized to the idea. I found the three published essays described below when I wasn't really looking for them; search the archives at the websites to find them if they fit your needs, but they are examples of what is available. They served our theme, and my Standards of Learning (SOL) goal.

Early in the pursuit of the geography theme mentioned above, I noticed a Lance Morrow essay in *Time* (October 30, 1989, p. 100), "When the Earth Cracks Open." It was printed in two not-so-neat columns. The margins were irregularly jagged to make a gash down the center of the page like an abyss, a result of an earthquake. And it was wonderful for teaching allusions. There were references to scripture, Moby Dick, Seneca, Albert Einstein, even Odysseus and his men.

Mr. Morrow referred to Shakespeare's play *Hamlet*, calling an earthquake "simply an unannounced convulsion. It is nature performing a Shakespearean tragedy," and described the fifth act of the play when, "after 15 seconds, Hamlet and the others lie dying, the stage is covered with blood and debris." He likens that to living for years on the San Andreas fault and joking about it. Who would have expected literary allusion in a geography-centered essay?

For primary source reading representing nineteenth-century style, you cannot find a better sample than the *Washington Post*'s story sharing a memoir of the great-great-great-grandfather of Alice Skelsey of

Annandale, Virginia. Hurricane Hugo had hit the bridge to Sullivan's Island the week before, reminding Miss Skelsey of her ancestor's journal entry, "This Scene of Destruction & Dismay, A Carolina Memoir: The Hurricane of 1822." She sent it to the *Post* where I read it and clipped it for use in class (Manigault 1989).

For older students, the *Smithsonian* magazine is another treasure trove for nonfiction writing that connects with geography and history, cultural activities, archaeology, and great biographies in science and social studies. The March issue for 1990 had Barbara Holland's article with the catchy title, "Vespucci Could Have Been Wrong, Right?" (p. 164). Most middle school and high school students would connect with this short paragraph written, tongue-in-cheek, about Columbus: "Isabella, his main fan, died. The nutmegs weren't nutmegs. . . . Folks began to wonder about the whole project." I censored it slightly, since there is no need to share with young students the "girl in every port" philosophy in the sentence, "The friends of his sailors started coming down with unsocial diseases that were new in Europe and a nasty surprise." In high school, that would be a marvelous opportunity to bring up social responsibilities.

Magazines for younger children can help with factual articles. *Ranger Rick* is the publication that comes to mind immediately. Check offerings from *Highlights for Children*. Its website is www.highlights.com. Is anyone without a website these days?

While students are reading and discussing the ideas from the theme shared with social studies, you can weave in literary topics like character development (see figures 5.2 and 5.3), setting, and even stylistic elements like literary allusions. You cover English and social studies bases at the same time with more firepower.

Other Arts of Language

Bookworms want to crawl through and nibble everything on a shelf in a library or a used bookstore, even the independent shops and chain stores offering brand-new publishers' releases. They either have a gene for this voracious appetite, or they learned it under the tutelage of a loving parent, a wise teacher, or a gifted librarian. We hear the flippant adage, "Use it or lose it." That goes for reading too.

CHARACTERIZATION

Figure 5.2.   Concept Pattern for Characterization

CHARACTERIZATION

Authors use various techniques to develop the characters for their readers. We call this writing skill CHARACTERIZATION and have identified five kinds of information authors supply to reach this goal of making their characters seem like real personalities.

Find pages in your fiction book where this information is given to you. Quote the sentences or phrases by filling them in the chart and give the page/s as your source.

CHARACTER INFO:	QUOTED EVIDENCE	PAGE
PHYSICAL APPEARANCE		
WHAT THE CHARACTER SAYS AND THINKS		
WHAT OTHER CHARACTERS SAY ABOUT HIM OR HER		
ACTIONS AND INTERACTIONS		
INFORMATION GIVEN BY THE AUTHOR		

Figure 5.3. Chart for Characterization Traits

Many specific mental skills are never developed by students who resist the Sirens' call to the world of books. Their imagination suffers, inferences aren't made when they do read, and they only have a conversational vocabulary. My readers can think of still more sad results of *not* reading. I do not want to discuss the currently popular graphic novels, but I suspect that they provide the scenes and the emotional facial expressions the reading novice's imagination cannot. TV does it for us? Help is at hand. Curiosity about a research topic can get students involved where nothing else has worked. Library skills help in a future pursuit of an education as well.

We've looked at projects and readings that connect well with social studies themes. Compositions in the style of reports, essays, and creative writing options can be formal assignments, or their elements can be worked into other projects. In most cases, the topics will relate to the theme in some way. When a written report is assigned, teachers can schedule trips to the library where they can oversee the click-and-scan generation as they use the library's computers, or they can hope to guide students into the *stacks,* or see that they practice their note-taking skills. Printing out the computer encyclopedia's article to highlight later is not really the same thing.

Note-taking and outlining, and compiling citations and bibliography references, can be joined by less pedantic and more real-world skills of daily recordkeeping, observing, interviewing, developing and taking surveys, and analyzing data. Computer programs exist for outlining, but I keep hoping students will have firsthand experience with the old-fashioned way first. How else do you learn why we keep those outline sections lined up if a computer is doing it for you? In addition, physically lining up main topics and indenting supporting points trains the eye and the mind to remember there are relationships being created that way.

These research skills can be taught and used by children of all ages and stages, as long as the materials are developmentally or age appropriate. Young children's research sources on nonfiction topics are marvels of condensed, clear information with wonderful illustrations; I used to tell my elementary education majors in Beirut, Lebanon, who also spoke Arabic, Armenian, and French, that they should get a children's book on the subject to get a basic understanding of their course's study topic in English.

On a recent trip to the Kennedy Center's gift shop in Washington, DC, I saw perfect examples of this point. A husband and wife team, Peter and Cheryl Barnes, wrote and illustrated books on each of the three branches of our government: *Woodrow, the White House Mouse* (1998); *Marshall, the Courthouse Mouse: A Tail of the U.S. Supreme Court* (1998); and *House Mouse, Senate Mouse: How Our Laws Are Made* (1996). Settings are drawn in accurate, historical detail; the mice replicate the human activities in our capital admirably. Children can see how a law dictating a certain cheese to be nibbled only on a specific weekday is declared unconstitutional.

Oral Skills: Don't All Students Have Too Many of Those?

If you have taught a class of congenial students of any age, you know that keeping talking in class under control is a disciplinary skill teachers must develop from the start. But being fluent in everyday conversation doesn't exactly prepare you for life as an adult. You need to have the confidence, the background knowledge, and the skill to express yourself in public, at town meetings or meetings of your organizations, perhaps even being on the podium yourself and addressing an audience.

If you reach an executive or managerial position in your life's work, you need to communicate clearly but politely with coworkers and subordinates. Only our bigwigs have access to teleprompters, and we all know it can be boring when we are read to from a text. Where is the lively interchange, the facial expression, the inflection, and most of all, the eye contact? How do we get to know the speaker when his personality is hidden behind a sheaf of papers, or he is continually looking down at them?

There is a reason why kindergarten and first grade teachers have show-and-tell to start their day. Early speaking experiences in a classroom get students ready for more sophisticated formats by building their confidence and giving them the chance to get used to talking *to* their classmates rather than talking in class. Theme-related opportunities to speak to classmates can start with a simple demonstration, how to do something, and build toward expository speeches, persuasive speeches, even debates across the grades.

Any time an oral speaking assignment is given, review with the students what keeps them interested in a speaker, and what causes them to start thinking about something else. Build a concept of what "a speech" is and post a visual, a representation of that generic model in the classroom (see figure 5.4).

Groups Speak

Remember that anything an individual speaker can do, a group can present as well. The task of sharing the message or the information can be divided among the members of the group, performed in skits, or even dramatized by several actors. Steve Allen, the late producer, musician, and comedian from the twentieth century, had a wonderful program on public television called *Meeting of Minds*. The scripts are now available in four volumes representing the series telecast for four seasons (1989).

Allen had four actors represent four famous people of history, but not necessarily those who were contemporaries. They were invited to dinner on the set. The ensuing conversation pitted such impossible combinations as President Theodore Roosevelt, Queen Cleopatra, Father Thomas Aquinas, and pamphleteer Thomas Paine for the very first program. Upper elementary students through high school might try the panel format. Give them specific instructions and class time to meet and prepare at least two questions for each of the other panel members.

Presenters can have a simple prop, wear a representative hat or jacket, or be fully costumed. At the simplest level, line up four desks, and have students make their own nameplates. Obviously this works beautifully for biographical subjects, but student panels can address any topic and share the crucial information about it. Students like the shared planning, and feel "there's safety in numbers." You'll read about these panels again in the discussion of the government theme of chapter 8.

Dare We Mention Grammar?

You bet we're going to mention grammar. Students who do not know English grammar have no way to transfer that understanding to the grammar of a foreign language they might study later. We cannot depend on translators every time our diplomats, business folk, and charity workers

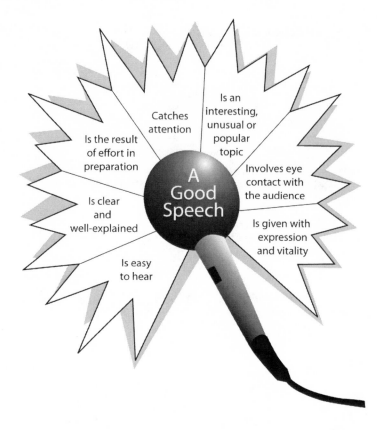

	Goal	Step 1	Step 2	Step 3	Step 4	Step 5
T A S K	To give a good speech,	pick a topic,	gather information,	organize notes as reminders of important points,	prepare an outline, and visual aids, if needed,	practice giving your speech.

Figure 5.4. Concept Pattern for a Speech Presentation

go abroad. We are in desperate need of bilingual people to deal with the other nations with which we share the earth. You can't start too soon with Standard English. Have you observed how people, even some highly educated people, talk on television?

Relating theme topics to grammar lessons is not as far-fetched or difficult as you might think. Consider first, however, grammar itself. Young children can learn name words and describing words, action and being words, and words (conjunctions) that hold phrases and thought pieces (clauses) together. You can add the official terms later as they mature.

I have mentioned that I consider this book a companion to my first book, *Brain-based Teaching for All Subjects.* There I describe a way to use closed shapes, symbols, to identify words as being one or another of the eight parts of speech. Because the brain notices closed shapes before other text fragments, symbols are a basic, easy way to work with grammar and young children.

To relate grammar lessons to various themes, raid student library books at the matching grade levels, or check out the reading series for the articles and stories that fit your theme. We always read a book in class that related to the theme. Here is yet another example of a link to the social studies geography theme from a novel for children ten years old and older. Note the underlined words. The first two paragraphs of Will Hobbs's *Downriver* begin:

> <u>I</u> <u>stumbled</u> <u>on</u> a rock that <u>was</u> barely sticking <u>up</u>, my <u>legs</u> were that <u>tired</u>. Flailing <u>for</u> <u>balance</u>, with the pack working against <u>me</u>, I slipped in <u>the</u> mud <u>and</u> almost <u>went</u> <u>down</u>. I <u>still</u> couldn't believe <u>this</u> was really happening. I couldn't believe <u>my</u> <u>dad</u> had <u>done</u> this to me.
>
> For <u>five</u> days <u>Al</u> had been leading <u>us</u> <u>into</u> the most <u>rugged</u> corners of the <u>San Juan Mountains</u> in southwestern Colorado, coaxing and pushing us over the passes and into the peaks, <u>through</u> good weather and bad weather, <u>but</u> mostly through <u>bone-freezing</u> rain and sleet. "<u>October</u> in the mountains," Al said with <u>a</u> grin. "You <u>live</u> a whole lot <u>closer</u> to the edge" (1992, p. 1).

Now picture those underlined words with numerals in parentheses before each one. On a lined piece of notebook paper, students numbered from one through thirty-three, and labeled each numbered word for its part of speech in that context. The test was definitely geographic, in having its setting in the Grand Canyon on the Colorado River, and it required students to use their understanding of grammar. Running down a list of labels saved grading time, too.

For the same geography theme, students read folktales from different language groups, and I had just happened to have an appropriate parts-of-speech quiz in my files. One summer, I had interned with an English teacher and supervisor in a nearby county. She was joining the faculty of the school of education on a state university campus. She asked me to go through her files and leave what I thought her replacement would be able to use, and by the way, take copies of anything I could use.

I found her original creation about the English folktale "Goldilocks and the Three Bears." Only this time I typed the text on every other line, underlining the words I was testing and putting them in boldface type. Then I went back and put in numbers above each word on the spaces I left between lines.

Once upon a time there were three little bears who simply had no adequate notion as to how they could stay out of trouble. Who knows? Maybe they meant to stir up that ruckus. Perhaps they acted weird because they had a deprived childhood or something. Then again, maybe it was just a terminal case of the munchies that drove them into the house of the kid with the yellow hair and abominable name.

Nope! That's it! I'd never really seen it before, but what was wrong was that the bears were merely curious, as all self-respecting cubs would be. And when they learned that there was some kid who had a name like Goldilocks living not too far away, well, they just had to take a little jaunt and find out what this kid's parents looked like.

Wouldn't you want to take a gander at some adults who had so little judgment as to name a kid Goldilocks? Hortense is even better than Goldilocks. What chance would you figure this kid has at a career with a handle like that? Who's gonna pay attention to a physicist with such a tag?

And can you imagine how long she'd last as a first year teacher when the kids found out what her first name was? Just about the only conceivable career choice she could make is being a beautician and hoping that Shirley Temple comes back into vogue. You gotta figure that little Miss "Good Ship Lollipop" wouldn't mind having Goldi fix her locks. But of course the best laid plans of mice and bears often get fouled up, and

<u>this</u> wasn't <u>destined</u> to be a good day for the cubs. In fact it was a <u>zinger</u> (Tomlinson 1990, used with permission).

That is quite a test—to say nothing of a piece of writing with allusions, and dialect, slang, and being an example of a parody on the *genre* of folk literature. And it brings up the memory of Brothers Grimm and their story-collecting project while traveling around nineteenth-century Germany. Folktale collections are a staple in all societies.

One of my files has a clipping, yellowed with age, probably not having been printed on acid-free paper, describing some poetry that teacher Elizabeth Huff's sixth graders wrote based on a recipe using the parts of speech. Their school was Hillsville Intermediate School here in Virginia, and from some photo captions on the back of the page, the publication may have been reporting on a conference meeting in "Region V." I can find no other data to reference this. If you recognize the teacher and the school, do let me know.

The pattern involved:	An example:
Line 1—article + noun	A desert,
Line 2—adjective + conjunction + adjective	arid and barren,
Line 3—verb + conjunction + verb	creeps and spreads
Line 4—adverb	frighteningly,
Line 5—noun, related to the first noun.	Wasteland.

More Geography with a Grammatical Purpose

When I was teaching we had access to the 1978 edition of *Grammar and Composition: First Course* by John Warriner et al. I am fairly sure that series was the source for sets of sentences I used for various themes. There was a set about Shakespeare's life. When social studies classes focused on the western frontier and our theme was frontiers (historical, social, and personal), we found out about the Donner Party.

The ten sentences were very discreet about that 1846 trek west. No mention of cannibalism appears; one sentence says, "Tamsen Donner's husband became very ill." The next adds that she chose between him and her children. She sent them on with the rescue team and stayed with her dying husband. She died too, but the children made it to California.

There's a grammar test with true historic drama. Do search for a film of this tragic story, or check out the film from PBS-TV's *American Experience* program. It is worth the effort.

Another frontier that grammar sentences addressed was Antarctica, its climate, and Robert Byrd's exploration. It was quite a frontier, too, and one of unusual challenges that could also have helped with the geography theme if one were pressed for material.

When working with clause patterns and sentence complements, I was delighted to find a set of sentences about the mountain ballad of "Barb'ry Allen," which included the information that ballad hunters have found ninety-two versions of that folk song in the state of Virginia alone. Grammar linked an early frontier and a famous folk song, or ballad. And the song tells an amazing story of death due to a broken heart. Just keep your eyes open, and possibilities for studying the English language without leaving your theme behind will be numerous to say the least.

One resource for grammar study that helps with thematic teaching has been around for decades, but it is *tried and true*, and still in print. Check the Internet for Phoenix Learning Resources, or use the grade-leveled workbook title *Keys to Good Language* (Culp 1982) on your browser. My elementary school colleagues and early middle school teachers liked this set of workbooks—don't boo or hiss! They have their place.

These workbooks are a gold mine for English teachers looking for sentences to teach grammar. All of the pages have not simply sets of sentences with models of a grammar structure or element, but the sets all have topics. You can find sentences relating to just about anything: history, geography, science, mythology, health, sports, travel, and more.

An Aside: Art Will Crop Up Everywhere If You Are Alert

By the way, American landscape artist William Keith (1838–1911), painted, in oil on canvas, a view of the *Donner Pass*. In my files, I have cut out a print of the painting that was advertised in a real estate magazine I picked up in Middleburg, Virginia. That was a most unlikely source, but there it was. Surely an art book would reference the painting. My copy of *American Landscape Paintings* did not, however.

Wrapping It Up

This past summer, the summer of 2008, a *Newsweek* issue had Sharon Begley's brain article about learning more while you figure out how to tell it to others. I never did unearth that *Newsweek* issue reporting on increasing children's understanding, but I was amazed to find the research reported in the fall 2008 issue of *Ideas in Action*, published by Vanderbilt University, Peabody College. Assistant professor of psychology, and lead author of the study, Bethany Rittle-Johnson (2008) reported results of research the team had published in the July issue of the *Journal of Experimental Child Psychology.*

The study examined whether explanation is useful when children under the age of eight apply what they learned to a similar task. Mothers were instructed simply to listen to the child's explanation. Researchers knew working with a peer or parent helped learning, but they wanted to test whether children were getting feedback and help that would explain the improvement. They found that by simply listening, mothers help their children learn.

Now, consider how much more opportunity children have for explaining their thinking or their problem solving when involved in the activities of a thematic curriculum. I hope this chapter gave you some additional ideas for involving students in thematic studies.

CHAPTER SIX

SIMULATIONS: DO-IT-YOURSELF AND READY-MADE

Have you ever heard a teacher say about a class, "Whew! There must have been something in the water that year"? There will be a type of group chemistry that acts as a catalyst in any mix of student personalities. The group will require a lot of energy and discipline in some cases. In others, things just seem to work well: students get excited about what they are doing, and if someone seems to be an irritant for one reason or another, the others seems to bring that student along, if not immediately, then eventually.

A class that fit the latter description inspired me, around the middle of the year, to try a Middle Ages simulation that I had read about in an issue of either *Instructor* or *Teacher Magazine*. A teacher had shared the way she organized her students, first as serfs on medieval manors, and then, based on their scores on texts and quizzes each week, they could advance through the ranks of that pyramid society toward the level of knights, and nobles, even the king. I decided to take the do-it-myself approach.

Simulations do just what the term implies; they simulate real life, and require group effort to re-create the setting in time or place. There was something about basing student advancement in a role-playing situation on their quiz and test scores that bothered me, so I didn't pursue that approach. I had students draw straws at one point, but basically they all worked together on whatever we were doing. At first there were the manor groups to deal with.

Simulations Require Organization

Grouping students can be touchy. They know each other pretty well by the middle of the year. If someone has not been doing the work, or has handed in poor or incomplete work, students who want to achieve at high levels do not want to be dragged down by a group member who will not take responsibility. Parents do not like a situation where their child reports to them about receiving a lower grade than usual on a group project because a classmate did not meet expectations.

But if you let students, themselves, sign up for groups, imbalances inevitably occur. Some students may try to sign for a group that is already up to size, or be disappointed they didn't get their choice. Some students are unsettled about working in groups to begin with, and want to be with at least one or two of their friends. Problems are hard to avoid, but where situations might create competition between groups as well as worries about individual grades within the group, it is best if teachers create the groups for a start.

I considered the boys first, thinking of lords, knights, and stewards before considering the girls for the feminine roles. There was no sign of liberation for women in the Middle Ages. That is when the command, "Get thee to a nunnery" originated, no? Marriages might be arranged, and widows often chose to live in a convent when something happened to their husbands. Wasn't that a great opportunity to compare and contrast the topic of gender roles then and now?

The Middle Ages through Projects, Art, and Dance

A bulletin board labeled "Nobles of Manor D" displayed a heraldic shield, and a parchment facsimile listing Lord Jon, Lady Mandy, Knight Sir Scott, Clergy Sister Wendy, Merchant Mistress Tracey, Freedman's Mistress Lori, and Freedman's Mistress Karen. I'm sure each manor had its own display board. We posted bestiary pages, illuminated letters with animal names; an explanatory posting read, "Monks in the Middle Ages became bored copying manuscripts, and entertained themselves by making a Bestiary."

Students built tabletop manors out of cardboard, with walls and various elements like castles, chapels, serfs' thatched roof cottages, and fields where they would rotate crops. One castle even had a lowered drawbridge. Students created dolls in costume to represent the roles they were living vicariously. They used empty soda pop bottles—perhaps weighted with sand or pebbles—with Styrofoam heads to create the body they clothed as their own characters on the manors. Naming the manors was a very serious decision for each group. Two winning names were Westerfield and Knight's Cross.

A crumpled paper, aged with cold tea, representing vellum, displayed a poem about the call to the Crusades written with illuminated letters. The Crusades poem was posted next to a chart titled, "Book ov Curtasye: kindly heed these rules ov Etyquett." The first rule says, "Gueysts myst have nayles cleane or they wylle disgust theyre table companyones."

Alas, there is no citation for the source of those nine rules, but a group of madrigal singers at the local conservatory performed medieval Christmas dinners, and the courtesy rules were probably part of one of their programs. And as mentioned in chapter 2, one of the madrigal singers came after school one day to teach the lords and ladies how to dance to the "Earl of Salisbury's Pavane." We ended with a banquet and knighting ceremony; we weren't picky about the fact that *pavanes* were popular dances in the mid-sixteenth century, a little late for our Crusade period. A *pavane* was a really old dance. That was enough. You can't have everything.

Readings Help to Re-Create Life from Eight Hundred Years Ago

Our reading series had an excerpt from the legend of Robin Hood and another short story based on the legend of Roland and Oliver. Two assigned book reports focused on historical fiction, set in the Crusade era through the Middle Ages, but not including the Renaissance. Students chose from the books culled for me by the librarian, and we all read Marguerite de Angeli's *The Door in the Wall*. Such a wealth of history and vocabulary was in that book.

My worn paperback copy still has a paper folded in it that says, "As you read *The Door in the Wall*, what do you find out about . . . ?" And then for pages 7–17, I have six questions beginning with (1) . . . a boy's training for knighthood? (2) . . . the way people got their names? (3) . . . the services a monastery or abbey provided? (4) . . . the jobs people had? (5)

. . . the problems travelers faced? (6) . . . what the problem was in London [at that time]?

The cover of a paperback copy of *Merry Ever After*, written by Joe Lasker, describes the book as a "Story of Two Medieval Weddings," a rich merchant's daughter married to the son of a noble lord, and the daughter of a blacksmith married to a village plowman. The contrast is fascinating, yet both marriages were arranged, and the illustrations are in the style of the period artwork one sees in museum halls.

I was almost sorry to be retired when *Good Masters! Sweet Ladies! Voices from a Medieval Village* (Schlitz) won the Newbery Medal in 2007. Were I still in the classroom at the appropriate grade level to be teaching the Middle Ages, the book would be perfect for student monologues. Each student would become a member of an English manor in 1255. With costumes, or just headdresses or hats, and a prop or two, classmates would have a complete view of village life.

Consider the Writing Possibilities Developing from the Readings

That word, *writing*, echoed in my mind as I typed. Teachers talk a lot about writing, they teach writing, they assign writing, they make distinctions between types of writing: creative, poetry, or expository. I am thinking the term probably triggers ideas like spelling and paragraphs for students, but in the computer age, they don't think much about penmanship.

If you have taught students the concept of the paragraph (Laster 2008), you can develop that concept into the dimensions of essays and stories. After reading a few items from a reading series, or from clippings you find in accessible material like age-appropriate children's books, or even *Reader's Digest* articles, students begin to get the idea of putting paragraphs together to tell longer stories, or explain more about a topic they were assigned. Post a concept pattern like figure 6.1.

Students who *live with* materials they see every day internalize them without knowing it. Sometimes they even make connections between two posted charts, for example, pinned up at different times but related in a way. A student, one day, announced she had seen a relationship between the posted paragraph pattern and the posted outline pattern next to it: topics and supporting points. The brain has a powerful imaging system.

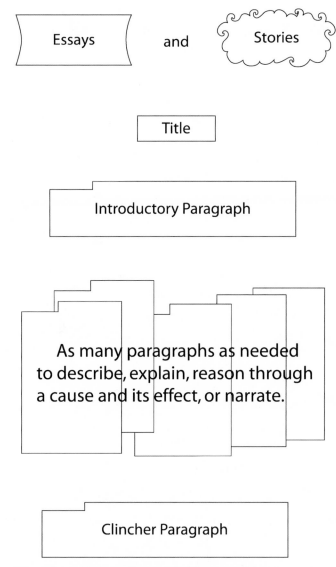

Figure 6.1. Concept Pattern for Essays and Stories

Having read *The Door in the Wall*, or any of a number of other books set in the Middle Ages, students have models for writing their own historic fiction and poetry. They might write an additional adventure for a character in a book, or the lyrics to the song a troubadour might perform as he traveled from manor to manor, or fief to fief. Journals following the

"A Day in the Life of . . ." pattern would be ideal for recording the activities of their lives as manor folk. The monologues in *Good Masters! Sweet Ladies! Voices from a Medieval Village* would set a wonderful example.

Dramatizing Medieval Situations

Role-playing in a simulation is drama itself. Before we actually tried a simulation of life in medieval times, we produced a play instead. An old reading series had a script version of a Margaret Leighton story still available in print, with eleven others set in medieval settings, if you look for it. The story was "Twelve Bright Trumpets." It describes a robber baron threatening the castle of a young woman whose brother is away on the Crusades. It involves a package of bulbs the brother sends from the Holy Land, and the bulbs' blooming in time for the brother's return, announced by herald trumpets just before the baron lays siege to the family castle.

One school year we actually performed it as a play, complete with costumes and minimal scenery. Another year students made puppets and performed the play as a puppet show, reading the script behind the created stage. I went so far as to take slides of the scenes and had students record the script in case there was a year when time didn't permit all the preparation for a full performance. The students could at least see a performance that had been given once. That actually saved time to try others things I'd discovered.

Visual Aids of Varying Types

- At the time, teachers could ask the library to arrange for a set of fifteen-minute films by *Encyclopedia Britannica* treating four topics pertinent to the Middle Ages.

- By the early 1990s, there was the *Castle: Siege and Conquest* game on a computer disk, as mentioned in chapter 1.

- David Macaulay's book *Castle* (1977) was a winner. Macaulay hosted a public television program, based on his book, which won an award. That VHS tape, at the time, was available for purchase via pbs.org. *Castle* is available now in DVD format.

- The plastic replicas of tomb carvings in British cathedrals give students the experience of doing rubbings without the expense of traveling. Those were on sale in the bookstore of the National Cathedral in Washington, DC.

The number of books available to enhance the material in the social studies textbook was staggering. Wonderful things have come out since. Other things just popped up along the way, for example, the plastic tomb-carving replicas.

Just don't ask me what we ate at the banquet and knighting ceremony. But it was finger food—probably bread, cheese, and dried fruits.

When a Field Trip Fits

Our small city is an hour and a half's drive from the nation's capital depending on traffic conditions. I would be remiss if I omitted describing a field trip that was a winner with everyone. When the guidance counselor found I was taking my class to Washington, DC, to the National Cathedral and the Islamic Center, she pointed out that we should see the Shrine of the Immaculate Conception, a Catholic basilica-style church with mosaics and gold on the inside of the huge dome that rivaled those in Ravenna, Italy.

The Islamic Center was a take-off-your-shoes experience in a beautiful edifice with the swirling artistic tiles one associates with the King's Mosque in Esfahan, Iran. There is nothing like firsthand experience. But the main purpose of the trip was to see the National Cathedral, built by craftsmen and stonemasons from Italy and our own country, and in good Gothic tradition, gargoyles and everything else.

The class had seen the public television video special *Cathedral*, based on the book by David Macaulay (1981). As we exited our chartered bus and headed for an entrance, we passed a posted map, the kind that tells you "You are here," and a young lady in the group gasped, "It *is* in the shape of a cross!" School boards need to keep the costs of field trips in their budgets. We all have places close to us that should be seen in person. Whether working out a simulation on your own, or using a ready-made simulation, field trips serve to supplement the integrated experience students are having.

Ready-Made Simulations

Everyone is so busy these days that the idea of planning a simulation around a theme is more than a bit off putting. In the last quarter of the twentieth century, we had computers, but no Internet sites out in cyberspace. Teachers used to check their mailboxes for notes, memos, announcements, handouts, letters, but they also found the catalogues we find so ubiquitous today. We discovered a catalogue one day that had some tempting topics with even more tempting descriptions for classroom learning.

I have already mentioned the first two—*Galaxy: A Space Odyssey*, and the Middle Ages simulation based on the pyramid structure of society. After using those two, we were hooked because of the enthusiasm of the students. Their depth of involvement was infectious; they were learning as never before. We went back to that catalogue for several other simulations while we were a team. You who are teaching today can find a plethora of available material.

This brain-friendly approach to learning and memory that we call thematic teaching is the way to develop students' intellectual backgrounds. Use "thematic teaching" as your search phrase. Select as many websites as you have time for, and you will find sites that share the philosophy and goals of this approach, plus references and available simulations. Teachers' blogs are places where you can read, comment on, and question what teachers have shared about using themes in their classrooms. Book sites like Amazon.com will respond to a "thematic teaching" search with some theoretical and some practical titles.

That friend of long standing used themes in primary grades, and recommended a website for the Buck Institute for Education (bie.org). At the home page, select the Project Based Learning tab. On that screen, go to PBL-Online and select "Designing Your Project" to find good things to think about when planning a unit. But scan the whole site for all it offers. Any search will include companies that have ready-made simulations and theme units for purchasing, which are worth checking carefully before making a purchase for your class.

Traditional print publications for teachers, like *Instructor* and *Teacher Magazine*, which also have websites, still share teaching ideas in various forms. Check your state's education association and its publication. I ran across some clever ideas, like a "Linguistic Autobiography" writing project, in a *VEA Journal* (the Virginia State organization of the NEA).

Educational Leadership and *The Kappan* have always been excellent sources for articles on trends and research in education, teaching, and learning. The former is the journal for the Association for Supervision and Curriculum Development and regularly publishes books on educational topics; the latter is a publication of the education fraternity, Phi Delta Kappa.

The simplest research device for finding good teaching activities and themes to develop is just a walk through classrooms in your own school building, or try bringing up the topic for conversation in the teachers' lounge—assuming you have time to get there now and then, sit down for a while, and actually discuss a teaching idea with a friend and colleague.

Extending Ready-Made Simulations to Suit Your Needs

When my colleague and I used published simulations, technology was still called *audiovisual aids*, and included film projectors, filmstrip projectors, opaque projectors, controlled readers, and overhead projectors; audio-cassettes and video cameras were available for taping. Simulations now involve computers for portions of a whole-class experience, and compact disks allow individual enthusiasts to play single-player simulations wherever they have a computer. All have their places.

I have searched the websites of what we knew as Interact of California (www.socialstudies.com and www.classroomscience.com), now several sites for social studies and science, even writing materials and simulations (including www.teachinteract.com, www.counselorresources.com, and www.writingco.com). Interact's reading contracts were wonderful sources of planned assignments and activities as well as reading lists in different categories of books. The websites still offer them. They still offer jury trial simulations and mock trials, too.

The interactive, ready-made simulation *Galaxy* no longer exists, which is a loss. Our students loved competing as space academy crews in space ships, even if it involved calculating distance in light-years. That simulation included five creative writing assignments involving the role that students adopted in the academy. They wrote in the first person according to prescribed situations. They designed spacecraft from various perspectives and made cutaway drawings. We added other activities to those in the simulation.

For language arts, students selected a random group of stars from the night sky and developed the origin myth to explain its appearance. They drew their constellation with dotted lines connecting the stars and a light sketch of the object or mythological character they imagined it to represent. For science class, they drew the constellation with colored stars to represent possible magnitude. It was a chart, accompanied by a written scientific explanation.

In the last theme of the sixth grade curriculum called Forces: Ecology and Environment, we used a simulation called *Ecopolis*. It involved taking a survey before and after being involved in the activities to check on possible attitude changes. *Ecopolis* took students through one hundred and fifty years of history in a fictional area of the United States, showing environment shifts that occurred as the population changed. It would be so apt for today's students. There is probably an up-to-date edition now.

In my search, now, in the twenty-first century, I found a simulation on the *First Transcontinental Railroad* and material on *The Donner Party*, both of which would support a theme on frontiers or the westward movement.

When the social studies curriculum was reorganized to help raise Standards of Learning scores in Virginia, I found myself leaving behind the Eastern Hemisphere and ancient history, and moving to modern. We carried on with an extension of the fifth grade U.S. history program.

One simulation called for posting a bulletin board–sized map of a county in Oklahoma where students signed up for their "land rush" property, a hundred and sixty acres according to the Homestead Act. We probably rolled dice to determine the climate and harvest results. And the railroad came through, bringing settlers to create towns along the tracks where the steam locomotives took on water.

Students come up with ideas, too, like watching a film about an Irish boxer and his love interest who lined up on horseback at the Oklahoma state line in 1889 to make a mad dash for a plot of land. It was called *Far and Away* (1992). A classic DVD outlet probably has the movie available even today; after all, it starred Nicole Kidman and Tom Cruise. One of my students suggested we watch it in class. I suggested they could enjoy it at home with their parents, where they could eat popcorn.

In the middle of this discussion about ready-made simulations, you might be wondering how expensive these purchases will be. A most popular simulation re-creating an archaeologist's experiences is *Dig*. I know it was available in the early 1980s, and the middle school catalogue from www.socialstudies.com now lists it as revised in 1998, describing it as "A Simulation of the Archaeological Reconstruction of a Vanished Civilization." For $59.95, you receive thirty-five student guides of twenty-four pages and a fifty-three-page teacher's guide. They suggest it works with twenty-five to thirty-five players and is planned for three weeks. I remember some materials as reusable.

The least costly simulation in the catalogue, *The Underground Railway*, runs $39.95, whereas the most expensive one, *The Civil War*, costs $74.95. *The Underground Railway* involves the entire class for three hours. The latter is recommended for fifth through eleventh grade and has five cycles from which to choose, depending on topics and time available. It can run for seven class periods or as long as thirty-two. Wars are more costly than secret escape routes, perhaps, but both are intense experiences.

How Much to Simulate?

Everyone likes desserts, but no one would continue to like them if sweets were all that the menu offered. You would not, could not, finish one simulation and begin another the next school day. Most simulations are like centerpieces; they allow getting involved with the subject in a direct way, as though living in the period or the situation itself. But while the simulation is a five-day to two- to four-week focus, a lot of other activities, assignments, classroom experiences, readings go on as well. Occasionally a simulation encompasses everything you wanted to cover, and you employ that one with a sense of fulfilled responsibility.

Two particularly complete simulations worked well, both of which are still available at the websites supplied above: *Christendom* was the very involved re-creation of the Middle Ages already described as a team effort. The other I used myself in a social studies class after the walls were replaced in our middle school building. *The Romans* divided the class into six groups for the six main patrician families in ancient Rome.

Here is how the website www.socialstudies.com whets your interest: "During seven phases (called *vias*), students join a *gen* (a clan), acquire Roman names, complete cooperative exercises on Roman daily life, build wooden standards, use knucklebones with a *Forum of Roma* gameboard. . . ."

I am delighted that this simulation is still available. Students really enjoyed the chariot race in the *Circus Maximus*, moving the family group's chariot playing piece around what I recall as a paper race track according to correctly answered questions. We ended with a Roman banquet, arranging the desks for an open space in the middle of the room, and dining most probably on bread, dates, cheese, fruit, and olives. Depending on time, student maturity, and levels of enthusiasm, bedsheet togas would add a lot to the banquet.

These days it would probably be very easy to find a DVD of *Ben Hur*, a Hollywood classic with the late actor Charlton Heston driving a chariot race in the Circus Maximus. You wouldn't have to view the whole film, just the scene where the chariot race takes place. Timed appropriately for the simulation, it would be a perfect taste of the wilder side of Roman society safely observed.

Welcome to Ellis Island

A third simulation was *Gateway*, which is still available. It works beautifully as a culminating activity for the theme of immigration. Students take on the personae of various people who came through Ellis Island, and then you stage the Ellis Island experience in some large hallway or open area of your school. Students have mock passports or identification papers, you can bring in older students and parents to act as officials, and everyone wears a costume, even if it is only a long skirt with an apron and, on the girl's head, a kerchief.

When I took on this simulation, I was working with the third social studies teacher to be part of the core team in the three-year sequential program. I was still following the themes we had set up originally, but the social studies teacher found this simulation and suggested it. We worked on it together. And when the Ellis Island experience actually occurred, a former student appeared, dressed up as the Statue of Liberty (!) as our young immigrants went through the arrival lines. As it was our culminating activity, there were other class activities that came first.

There Are Frontiers to Cross:
Readings Are Vicarious Experiences

This was a particularly good second theme for the year because once the immigrants arrived at American shores, they often got on trains heading to other parts of the country. Robert Louis Stevenson sailed from Scotland and made a cross-country train journey in 1879 to see an ailing friend. He kept a journal, which Jim Murphy (1993) used to create his book, *Across America on an Emigrant Train*, complete with period photos and painting.

We had a class set of Murphy's book in a storeroom, so I assigned three or four students in a group to read and report on each of the six chapters. My copy still has a note reminding me that "next year, have students make postcards 'from RLS' as he might have sent them from the train journey."

Joan Lowery Nixon wrote the Ellis Island Series of books describing characters who represented the main groups of immigrants. They were a perfect resource for literary groups in this theme. Karen Hesse wrote *Letters from Rifka*, Sonia Levitin wrote *Journey to America*, and Elvira Woodruff penned *The Orphan of Ellis Island*. All serve the purpose of showing characters in the historic setting, and what it required of them to prosper in the face of obstacles.

An Ingmar Bergman film shows the sea voyage, arrival, and subsequent train ride of Swedish immigrants. Students see what it took to keep one's sanity, choose the land wisely, and invest the energy to clear it, farm it, and make the Minnesota wilderness produce. I believe he made two films from Vilhelm Moberg's four *Emigrant Novels*. His actors, Max von Sydow and Liv Ullmann, are the Swedish immigrants personified. The first film is entitled *The Emigrants*. You need see just that one.

Public television developed a series on the various hyphenated Americans as separate groups, but also a series on Ellis Island itself. You can access those in various ways, I'm sure, and don't forget the Broadway musical *Fiddler on the Roof* (1964), available as a film (1971). It tells the story of a Russian village in 1905 and how it was affected by the czar's edict. The second act ends with Tevye's family leaving for America where a cousin has settled already.

Depending on the age of your students, you might consider another movie that is available: Don Bluth's animated story of a family of mice who flee czarist Russia and emigrate on board a ship. In *An American Tail* (1986) the elements of the immigrant story are all portrayed, from persecution in Russia to hearing about the streets in American being "paved with cheese," and the conditions aboard the ship, not to mention the arrival in New York Harbor. The problems continue from there to the song lyrics of "Somewhere Out There."

Actually, I don't think student age is a problem. When you use material created with young children in mind, as an adult you are often amazed at what information is slipped into the story one way or another. Challenging older students to pick out the relevant information to the content you are studying often has them highly entertained while deeply engaged with actually thinking and analyzing. Disguised approaches achieve a lot.

Armed and Ready

Most teachers, actively working with students now, are armed with the skills needed to visit the blogs and the organization sites that pop up with the search phrase "thematic teaching." Colleagues and a former student now working in the field tell me that another search phrase, which might surprise you, is "expeditionary learning."

Teachers' stores carry products locally, but there is a myriad of sites online offering seemingly endless numbers of must-have resources and tools. I think the younger generations are going to evolve with brain filters that help them approach the overwhelming onslaught of choices. Perhaps there is value in the "Keep it simple, seriously" (KISS) admonition.

CHAPTER 7
SOME SUCCESSFUL
EXAMPLES FROM THE PAST

By now, it is obvious that students and educators were having a good time connecting themes with real-life learning experiences that made studying seem like play, but that didn't happen overnight. I had a colleague who had an amazing gift for coming up with those real-life learning experiences, yet teachers could adapt the lesson activities we used for working with both higher and lower grade levels. That is also true for the curriculum projects and topics in these last two chapters.

Back in chapter 2, discussing correlation and scheduling, I glibly introduced the themes for seventh and eighth grade. Now my aim is to discuss them more thoroughly so that you can almost see the year unfold. The first seventh grade theme was immigration, but we had to settle in first.

Begin Each Year with the Student—Reading Aloud

Each new school year is a transition period, and transitions have their hoped for joys as well as bringing with them some trepidation. Reading aloud for ten or fifteen minutes each day provides a settling routine for students coming in from the wilds of the hallway. In chapter 4, I referred to Jean Craighead George's *My Side of the Mountain*, a story about a runaway who goes to find his great-grandfather's abandoned farm. In sixth grade, it worked perfectly with students who felt lost in a huge new school with peers who were strangers. It represented survival, or the ecology theme. Had I been teaching seventh grade then, I would have used it there, too.

The book represents survival, yes, but also a personal frontier. Sam is in a quandary over whether he will follow his father and grandfather to sea, or prove that a Gribley could live on the land. It would be a good option for a geography theme or one on environment. Sam trains a falcon, talks about a weasel, muses on the effects of seasonal change on the hardwood forest and animals, to say nothing of his own potential survival. He hollows out a tree home, and tans the hide of a deer in the rainwater in a rotten oak tree stump. And yes, Paramount Pictures made a movie of the book years ago. Read it aloud and allow students to make their own mental movie.

Another gem, and one taking a mythical journey through the Lands Beyond to Dictionopolis, is *The Phantom Tollbooth* by Norton Juster. Juster makes creative use of all the quirks and beauties of the English language and, among other interesting regions in this inexplicable land, includes a stop in Digitopolis for the Mathemagician to share the wonders of numbers. The main character is an immigrant in the Lands Beyond.

The character, Milo, is searching his own frontier, but the language play makes this book perfect for starting a year when students might be writing their own "linguistic autobiography." *Tollbooth* works into the immigration theme, too, since family background plays a huge part in personal vocabularies. The *Virginia Education Association Journal*'s article about students writing about their own use of language would pair up well with this book. My search skills did not find archives at their site going back far enough to locate the article.

Esther Forbes's *Johnny Tremain* does a beautiful job of putting a personal face on the American Revolution even though our first theme in seventh grade was immigration in the nineteenth-century sense. Puritans and Pilgrims were immigrants, no? (See figure 7.1.) I handed out a procedure frame because the response was to be an essay, and students need to prepare as they read. There was no escape here.

Just be sure whatever you read has value for language, for life, and is thought provoking, one of my mother's favorite compliments. Teachers cannot look away from the importance of great characters, though. They make or break the book.

	GOAL	STEP 1	STEP 2	STEP 3	STEP 4	STEP 5
T A S K	To think and conclude about the novel, JOHNNY TREMAIN.	NOTICE, as you read, evidence for answering the various questions in the steps. You might write the topics on a 3x5 card and list the supports. When ready to draft your ideas, UNDERLINE the title on the top line, CENTERING author and pages on subsequent lines. SKIP a line before the text begins.	SUM UP, in an opening paragraph, the kind of life an apprentice led in colonial times. CONTINUE with a paragraph that explains why the Bostonites and farmers planned revolt and tell whether they are justified. Provide a transition into the next paragraph. (two paragraphs)	INTRODUCE Johnny into your essay. DESCRIBE how he "grows" as a personality by mentioning at least 3 different adjectives or character traits that show stages in his life. What events cause his "changing"? How was he influenced by Rab and Cilla? (one paragraph)	PROJECT Johnny's future if he lives through the war. At the book's end, Johnny is planning to join the Minutemen. If he survives, do you think he will claim his inheritance? EXPLAIN why you believe as you do. (one paragraph to conclude)	ASK a parent or friend unfamiliar with JOHNNY TREMAIN to read your essay. Make any changes necessary to have a clear, written discussion. Correct any errors and recopy if necessary.

Figure 7.1. Procedure Frame for *Johnny Tremain* Novel

September's Creative Writing:
Ask Students to Look into the Mirror

Team teaching or sharing ideas with colleagues can bring bonuses. Someone would run across a good idea, share it, and if it worked well, we would use it again and again until we got tired of it, or decided it had served its purpose. Students only had one shot at the work; in this instance, poetry books.

If you can do the assignments along with your students, creative writing is an eye-opener and lets students see into your mind as you see into theirs. Our poetry books had sections. Part I was called *Searching Within*, and three poems bore the titles "Earliest Memory," "Speaking to Memory," and "Dreams." Part II was titled *Sharpening the Senses* and had only two poems, one with the same name as the section, the other called "Image."

When you got to part III, *Who Am I?*, you had to consider yourself as other people saw you in "First Impressions," then "Self-Portrait." You hauled out the psychiatrist's couch for "Self as Other." What would you be if you weren't you? And "Self to Another" required addressing someone with whom you would like to share your thoughts if you could. But everything was more comfortable, even relaxing, in part IV, *My Personal World*.

The poem collection ended with part IV's poems on "Environment," "Favorite Place," "Family," and "Friend." As we completed a draft for the poem of the day, I would ask if anyone wanted to share theirs. If they didn't, I read mine, and usually others followed. We wrote a poem each day for the first three weeks of school, and then we crafted them into hand-bound books.

Bookbinding was a project my teacher mother had shared with me. It became an annual event in the classroom. Classmates made dust covers for each other's books, an experience in marketing and design modeled on dust covers the librarians supplied. Students had a new appreciation for books as they prepared covers, sewed quires of pages, fastened them into the prepared cover, and glued end papers down. Now there is a computer program to help every step of the way. The computer result looks more polished, but it isn't the same as when completely handcrafted. Still, students had pride in their work, and they will cherish the books for years.

A Grading Rubric

With a checklist form for grading the books, teachers may add points to a passing base of seventy, as there are twenty-five separate items to check for, or they may arrange the elements of the project on a continuum for a curve suggesting excellent, good, average or adequate, and fair or poor.

Example Evaluation Form

Bookbinding—Poem Books
>Cover:
>>Title_____
>>Author/illustrator_____
>>Design_____
>Binding Quality:
>>Quires stitched_____
>>Mitered corners_____
>>End papers_____
>Parts of Book:
>>End pages_____
>>Title page: Title_____
>>>Author/illustrator_____
>>>Design_____
>>>City_____
>Copyright on back_____
>>Dedication_____
>>Table of contents_____
>>Author information_____
>>Pagination, number of pages_____
>Poetry:
>>Neat, legible penmanship____
>>Correct spelling_____
>>Punctuation for meaning_____
>>Titles_____
>>Page format (layout)_____
>>Appropriate illustrations_____
>Poetry Content:

"Word pictures" _____
Unusual words, phrasing_____   Think: "Big Project!"

Name Acrostics—They Work for Almost Anything

A name acrostic works at any age and can involve self-knowledge or the findings of simple research. When sixth graders were new to middle school, it served to introduce them to their classmates and teachers. It adapted for a study of Greek and Roman mythology when the god's or goddess's name was designed and lettered down the middle of a vertically held piece of unlined paper, nine by twelve or fourteen inches. Statements about the deities were written through each letter so the letter was used to spell one of the words.

For the students' name acrostics, letters went down the left side of the page, drawn large, designed perhaps and colored brightly, spelling first and last names. The letters began the first word of an adjective, or a phrase or statement, about the student. In the seventh grade, the name acrostic (see figure 7.2) became one of the introductory pages in the hand-bound self-poems book. Or it was an opening page for the autobiography essays discussed next.

	GOAL	STEP 1	STEP 2	STEP 3	STEP 4
T A S K	To create a Name Acrostic to tell something about yourself.	Make a rough draft in pencil. Put the letters of your full name down the left side of the paper. Use each letter to start a word in a phrase that tells something about you. Talk to a parent if you need some ideas. They know you well, too.	On unlined paper, design the letters that spell your full name, and will attract notice when they are colored. You want your name seen first. Write the rest of each line in cursive. If you rule light pencil lines across the paper, you'll have straight lines to guide you.	Pick your favorite colors to make your name stand out. Color in the letters of your name neatly. Check your spelling. Did you copy your words or phrases correctly? Check for any missing words. Correct anything you need to. Remember to erase any pencil guidelines.	Put your finished work in a folder to protect the edges until you turn it in.

Figure 7.2. Procedure Frame for a Name Acrostic

Autobiography from a School Year's Perspective

Another "getting to know you" project that lasted for thirty or more weeks of the school year was a weekly composition on prescribed topics. All together, the compositions produced a fine autobiography for the student in that particular year of his or her lifetime. Again, experience with this writing project tells me to recommend that teachers write along with their students here too, but perhaps they might share only bits and pieces of their weekly essays. Save what you write for your grandchildren. Here are the weekly topics:

1. Before I Was Born (family members and setting)

2. I Made My Entrance (early years of life)

3. On My Birthday (what was going on in history)

4. The First Home That I Remember (complete with floor plan?)

5. Before I Started School (daily activities and memories)

6. Early School Years

7. The Outside World and Me (environment, immediate and distant)

8. Special Times (holidays and trips)

9. A Few Good Dates (as memorable days in the past)

10. My Family (parents, siblings, relatives)

11. Family Life (more memorable events or experiences)

12. Map of Life (outline map of the United States with dots identifying places lived and where relatives lived; include a key)

13. Being My Age (the student's age at the particular grade level)

14. Everyday Life at ___ (the age of the student at this writing)

15. Thoughts on Friendship

16. Love and Marriage (student's ideas of, or experience with)

17. Timeline (We often did personal timelines at the beginning of the year as a way to establish a social studies concept. Students were able to copy the timeline information into their autobiographies here.)

18. The Brag Page (things the student is proud of)

19. Life Messages (wisdom from others, from reading, from experience)

20. The World of Work (student odd jobs or career ambitions)

21. Who I Was . . . Am . . . Might Be (a look past, present, and future)

22. Likes and Dislikes (pet peeves, annoyances, favorites)

23. Thoughts on Serious Subjects (up for interpretation)

    Five things that would help my world

    Advice for other people

    In case of fire . . .

    The world's most pressing problem

    My most difficult problem

    My beliefs

    What puzzles me

24. Highs and Lows (Revisit the timeline, and re-create it, but plot a graph line rising and falling along the horizontal line—the one for the big events in the student's life and the nation—but representing relative emotional ups and downs. It looks like a line plotting the economic scene at some point in history.)

25. Who Am I . . . Really?

26. The VIPs in My Life

27. The Future (as the student sees his or hers)

Given the seven subtopics under "Thoughts on Serious Subjects," there were topics enough for the students to write throughout the school year on a weekly basis. They copied their proofread and edited essays in a lined journal, taking home what was a priceless possession, whether they knew it at the time or not. If funds are a problem, colored paper covers can serve for notebook pages held together with paper fasteners. The result is still a treasured keepsake.

Library Orientation with a Purpose

Students need to be introduced to the school's library and the librarians at the beginning of each school year no matter the grade level. It makes even better use of time if you have a secondary purpose for the trip too. After librarians point out the library facilities—where to check out books and return them, or locate stacks of fiction and nonfiction—and hold up some tempting titles, they usually turn students loose to look around. You can have other goals in mind.

We signed up for library orientation, and when the librarians finished their spiel, they helped the students research the meanings of their names. The link with immigration was obvious since family names usually represent the nation of origin of the first immigrant. Some names were respelled by Customs officials, as immigrants passed through Ellis Island. Students learned that some names have common links: Helen of Troy started it all with the Greek word for *light*, but depending on the modern language, Ellen, Nell, Elaine, and Ellen all come from the same root. Name meanings were written in the student autobiographies in journal form.

An excerpt from Laurence Yep's *Child of the Owl* called "My True Name" was a lucky find in the literature series at that time.

Interviewing an Immigrant

In this immigration theme, students interviewed immigrant families they might know here in their small Virginia city. That was an opportunity to stress preparation, what questions to ask, how to politely request the interview in the first place, and how to send a thank you note afterward. As an example, I had a copy of the experience of a Vietnamese pharmacist.

Her family had been sponsored by a local church. She wrote about the family's escape from that war zone, and it became our model of what the interviews might yield.

Biographies of Famous Immigrants

A video of Andrew Carnegie's life was available from a film collection for teacher use. Some students had heard of Carnegie Hall in New York City, but were unaware of his library projects. It was a good way to reinforce social studies classes and look at reasons people had for immigrating to the United States. Looking up the topic of immigration in a *World Book Encyclopedia* resulted in a long list of now famous immigrants. Our librarians found biographies in the library's collection for the students. Whether for a first visit or well into the academic year, the library and librarians remain a vital resource.

The librarians provided a list of thirty possible titles, from which I selected those that fit my purpose and had the most probable appeal for students, with three or four extra for "choice." A one-to-one ratio of books to students didn't provide any leeway, and I didn't want to punish the late arrival to the table. That reader would start out with a disgruntled attitude before opening the book.

Another videotape had focused on immigrants who come to America today. With that in mind, we developed a matrix to organize our findings from the biographies. We noted where the biography subjects came from and where they settled in the United States; what strong character traits did they seem to have; when did they immigrate and for what reason? We had columns for information, so we could generalize from them:

- Who They Were . . .
- From Where They Came . . .
- When They Came . . .
- Why They Came . . .
- What They Became . . .

The information formed a table when displayed on a bulletin board, much as facts about the planets of the solar system had worked in the sixth grade, displayed on a room-divider screen.

As this theme traveled along with the shifting immigrant groups and personalities, the librarians were picking the next fiction books about immigrants arriving in America. One year our immigrant fiction reading was done in small literature groups thanks to a donation from a parent who purchased the Ellis Island Series mentioned in chapter 6, and we saw the Ingmar Bergman film *The Emigrants*, also mentioned in the previous chapter.

Cultural Baggage a Loaded Term

Part of the culture that we share here in America is a familiarity with the image of the Statue of Liberty as a welcoming symbol in New York Harbor. Not everyone has visited it, but most everyone knows about it and the excerpt from the poem by first-generation Russian-American Emma Lazarus inscribed at the statue's base:

> Give me your tired, your poor,
> your huddled masses yearning to breathe free,
> the wretched refuse of your teeming shore.
> Send these, the homeless, tempest-tost to me,
> I lift my lamp beside the golden door!

("The New Colossus")

Students can hear those words performed by the Pennsylvanians, conducted by the twentieth-century's renowned choral director, Fred Waring. Irving Berlin set this text to music in the early part of the twentieth century, himself of immigrant background. Students will sense the different effects of poetry when used as song lyrics. This is a good time to pick appropriate adjectives to describe the feelings in the poem and the mood in the music.

A wonderful balance to Emma Lazarus's poem is that of Elias Lieberman, "I Am an American." The Lazarus poem brings the immigrants to this shore; the Lieberman poem describes how they assimilate from being "an atom of dust . . . a straw in the wind, To His Serene Majesty" to individually being "proud of my future. I am an American."

The wedding of poetry and music at this point suggests mentioning a song from a film that is discussed later in this chapter. In the musical

West Side Story the Puerto Rican character, Anita, sings "I like to be in America." It was almost an automatic reflex to ask students to write original poems on "What America Means to Me." And it was about at this point that we watched *An American Tail* as mentioned in chapter 6.

Films and photos of immigrants arriving at Ellis Island all include luggage grasped tightly: suitcases, cloth-knotted boxes, and carpetbags.

What's in the Baggage?

In small groups, students prepared mock-up suitcases containing articles that symbolically represented the major national cultures left behind, but were items that one might still treasure as a memory of their homeland. This baggage included keepsakes, souvenirs to keep as reminders from the Old World in their new homes. We did consider what we would pack as *our* cultural baggage should we ever emigrate for any reason.

Rounding Up the Theme

As we neared the end of the immigration theme, students worked in groups to put out newspapers covering a decade of time when immigration was at its height in the nineteenth and early twentieth centuries. (Refer to figure 6.1.) And we prepared the students for that prime example of culture clash, when new immigrants meet already-established groups: the film version (1961) of the Broadway musical *West Side Story*, with music by Leonard Bernstein and lyrics by Stephen Sondheim. How do you prepare for that experience?

We read a play version of the Greek myth of Pyramis and Thisbe. Lovers live side by side in Babylonian brick homes surrounded by walls. They communicate through a hole in the shared wall because their parents forbid their meeting, much less marrying. That should sound familiar. We then read a short, radio-version script of Shakespeare's *Romeo and Juliet*, to show that good ideas are sometimes new creations of old ones.

When we saw *West Side Story*, we were ready to watch the characters and find the parallels in the already-read versions, old truths clothed in new vestments. Cultural baggage, immigrant aspirations, the need to belong, conflicts between ethnic groups and their traditions: these were all there on the television screen. One year I heard sniffles at the death scene! And there was much meat for discussion that related to social studies classes.

After three or four years of using the immigration theme, we finally found the perfect culminating activity as described in the chapter on simulations. So just recall or actually look back to chapter 6 and find references to *Gateway: An Ellis Island Simulation*, still available from the website www.socialstudies.com. We all became immigrants going through Ellis Island.

The Immigrants Had to Go Somewhere, Didn't They? Frontiers to Cross

When my maternal grandfather got off the tramp steamer on which he worked his way over to America from what is now Prague, Czechoslovakia—yes, he traveled overland first to get to a seaport—he was approached by a man offering to train him to be a butcher. That became his future, which included owning a small store in connection with his meat sales, and being a respected leader in his community.

Where did other immigrants go if they had no relatives here already? In social studies class, the students were making their way through the post–Civil War period. It seemed as though everyone was pushing west across the Great Plains. Because these were often immigrants moving west for land and opportunities, students sometimes did not notice they were moving into the frontier theme and leaving the immigrant theme behind.

The Irish Potato Famine in the 1840s started the first real flood of ethnic immigrants. Most came from northern Europe at first, then southern and eastern. With the building of the transcontinental railroad in the United States, the need for labor brought Chinese immigrants to the West Coast. You can read Laurence Yep's *Dragon's Gate* (1993) for a vivid account of the dangerous, backbreaking labor required on the project that brought the coasts together and "grew" the middle of the country via railroad towns and cities. The whole book is jaw-dropping.

Another Laurence Yep excerpt from *Child of the Owl*, "Paw-Paw," was in the eighth grade literature book *Literature and Life*. In that story, a twelve-year-old Chinese-American girl faces several of the hurdles encountered by relatively recent arrivals to our shores—loss of parents, living with relatives, generational divides, and constant challenges from the new culture. Here was a geographic and historical frontier that was personal.

What Is a Frontier?

We took a broad view of frontiers, seeing them as geographical and historical, but also personal, and social too. Today we are familiar with expressions such as "pushing the envelope" or "pushing back the frontiers of science," or more specifically an area of science. Remember "Space, the final frontier" from the television series *Star Trek*? Land under the sea, and even the state of Alaska have been called last frontiers here on earth.

Someone gave a collection of Remington bronzes to our local university, where they were exhibited in the library. After seeing a PBS-TV video about the artist, students earned extra credit for a journal-type report of their visit to the exhibit, describing how they believed these pieces of art represented their mental image of the Old West.

PBS-TV added another serendipitous gift to the frontier theme. There was a biography of Willa Cather on the Washington, DC, channel, which was available on videotape. Cather had actually lived in a small town outside our city in the northern Shenandoah Valley, and moved west by train when her father moved the whole family to Nebraska. Her novel *My Ántonia* is autobiographical fiction. I remembered, fondly, reading the book in high school myself, and thought students would too. Some did. Some didn't, but it served our theme well. Here were Virginians going to Nebraska where different immigrant groups were mingling on the frontier. Who could forget the journey on the train, to say nothing of the Russian bachelor brothers? And then there were the adventures with various wildlife on the prairie—woodchucks and snakes, to name two.

Inspired by the book, the students interviewed their oldest living relatives and wrote up their findings in the way Cather used memories of her grandmother in the novel. I did caution them about phoning long distance without parental permission if an aging relative lived in California. Today's cell phones solve that cost problem with prepaid minutes. Students found out things about their families that they had not known, some new stories that even parents had not known.

The problem of immigrants lacking proficiency in English, which hindered understanding each other, led to a discussion first, and then to groups working on arguments, for or against, to answer the question, "Should English Be Our Official Language? Yes or No?" Students were going to read biographies again, this time about people who lived on a frontier in fields of knowledge, like science and inventions, or social problems, and regional activities. They would make speeches of five minutes in length, and each student would be responsible for responding in letters to two or three classmates' presentations.

The class drew names in case freedom to choose led to overresponding to a few students while others were overlooked. The directions suggested they find three positive things to say about the classmate's speech, and in addition make a suggestion to improve a future presentation. Teaching courtesy and diplomacy is as important to the future as knowledge.

Some other writing activities grew out of the Cather novel. When Jim Burden, another character, remembers Ántonia at the start of the book, students were asked whom they would remember, and then to write about their memorable person. PBS-TV, however, came through again. Following the copyright rules about taping from television and using the program within a week—teachers should check to be aware of the law—we saw a ten-minute segment from the *McNeil/Lehrer NewsHour* called "What is a 'typical' American?" That brief ten-minute news item was the thrust behind an essay on students' ideas about "What is an American?"

We were looking now at the character traits that were necessary to cross the various frontiers. Hollywood offered some dated but famous views of conquering the Old West in the film *How the West Was Won*. Social studies classes could critique the historic accuracy. And then we encountered that famous Midwest character, Samuel Clemens, known to us all as Mark Twain of riverboat connections.

Never Shalt Thou Not Meet Twain

Could we be in a frontier theme study and not read the nation's most famous author of all time? The answer is, of course, no. That superlative is probably still appropriate. Students read Twain novels in small groups. There was a television performance of Twain's "Diaries of Adam and Eve." I found "The Notorious Jumping Frog of Calaveras County" along with the "Mysterious Stranger" in *The Portable Mark Twain*, a hefty 786-page paperback (De Voto). High school and college courses include Mark

Twain in their syllabi. You might check with high school teachers to avoid duplication if you are a middle school teacher.

We wrote personal experience pieces a la Twain, and since Twain employs dialect spelling, and Cather's Jim Burden had told Ántonia not to "talk *bohunk*," students found dialect excerpts to read to the class. We tried to identify the locale of each reading, but needed help. We were not as astute as Professor Higgins (Lerner and Lowe, *My Fair Lady*), who could determine precisely a speaker's home in England. Using the concept pattern for a novel (Laster 2008), groups analyzed the Mark Twain novels they had read. Twain worked for some middle school classes; other options remain for younger students working in a frontier theme.

The second book in the Laura Ingalls Wilder series, *Little House on the Prairie* (1935), is probably the quintessential example of life on the nineteenth-century frontier that several generations of elementary school students have devoured already. Try to get students started reading the books before someone mentions the equally loved television series.

Blurring the Borders

We were subtly moving into the conflict and resolution theme with some final references to frontiers, where conflicts were inevitable between settlers, ethnic groups, Native Americans, extremes of climate, and the troubles presented by sheer distances. We had seen the Mexican-American War and the Civil War in the mid-nineteenth century, and the Spanish-American War was on the horizon by the end of that period. I chose portions of E. L. Masters's *Spoon River Anthology* to read aloud. Like Mark Twain, Masters responded to people he met, but in poetry form.

The anthology is a collection of poems about citizens of fictional Spoon River who are "sleeping on the hill" in the local cemetery. Considering that the opening poem mentions brothels, shameful childbirth, and thwarted love, I did not assign this book for class reading. I read selected poems for my own poetic purpose.

When I read the first poem, "The Hill," I skipped the inappropriate bits. In the next poem, "Hod Putt" is buried close to "Old Bill Piersol" and was tried and hanged for robbing and killing a traveler one night. After that I skipped to page 32. That page puts the spotlight on "Constance Hately" who raised her orphaned nieces, but never let them forget they depended on her. I read a total of seven poems written in the voices of seven people. Why? Students would apply this approach to Twain characters.

The groups of students who had read and analyzed Twain novels now selected four characters from their books and wrote Spoon River–like poems about those characters. We shared them and posted them on a bulletin board. Students at all grade levels could create poems written in the voice, or persona, of any book character. Conflict is a down-home topic of *Everyman*. Conflicts in small towns and cities find parallels in contemporary times. One has only to read the local newspaper to find them.

With Conflict Comes the Hope of Resolution

As we finished up frontiers, I assigned conflict fiction, with the librarians' help, and began reading aloud *Park's Quest*, Katherine Paterson's book about the son of a Vietnam War soldier who didn't return home. That was set in a Washington, DC, suburb and on a rural Virginia farm, almost home territory. This is an appropriate time to develop the concept of conflict itself, as being internal and external, as shown in figure 7.3. The war was an international conflict, but the feelings Park had about the father he never knew were personal conflicts that too many have felt in real life.

The library's copy of *Necessary Parties* by Barbara Dana, the wife of actor Alan Arkin, dealt with a father, in midlife crisis, who announces to his stunned children that he and their mother are separating. The book was well presented in video form too. In it, the son finds a book called *The Rights of Teens*. The fourteen-year-old learns that his father's mechanic is actually a disenchanted lawyer, and convinces him to bring a suit against the father. There was plenty of overt and internal conflict set, not close to, but literally in, the home. How did the people respond?

We started to notice how people react to conflict, how they deal with it. As the class read fiction set in times of historical conflict, they prepared to compare fiction versus facts from social studies class. In reading their own conflict fiction books, students kept a *persona journal* for the main characters, which they later shared with the class, sitting behind desks arranged in a circle for that purpose. Things stayed at a conversational level, and with that changed perspective, the interaction was interesting to

CONFLICT

It can be **INTERNAL** (inside of you);
It can be **EXTERNAL** (attacking from the outside).
SO: Who is the "enemy"?

Figure 7.3.   Types of Conflict in Fiction

watch. Admittedly conversation circles work better in smaller class groups, and not at all grade levels. Don't dismiss them completely though.

And then it was time to read Shakespeare. Unlike Twain, the Bard often got his ideas from older tales.

Conflict in Shakespeare

I read the class the Danish folktale "The Most Obedient Wife," which May Hill Arbuthnot calls "a most amusing variant of *The Taming of the Shrew* theme" (1952). I recall a similar tale set in the Appalachians where a farmer is taking his new wife up to his hillside farm. She berates him for his treatment of the horse when it stumbles. He repeats his behavior when the horse stumbles again, and shoots the horse the third time. When his bride objects strongly, he says to her, "That's once." Both stories are good introductions to *The Taming of the Shrew*.

The library had an audiocassette of a staged interview with William Shakespeare. PBS-TV had come out with a four-hour series called *In Search of Shakespeare*. The Royal Shakespeare Company is included in this biographical collage of interviews, important events and locations from the playwright's life, including the Globe Theater, and excerpts from his plays.

A *Frontline* series program, "Who Is Shakespeare?" (available on-line through pbs.org), highlighted a group in England that believes the plays were written by a nobleman, an earl who wouldn't be identified in public. The adherents to that theory felt a small town glove-maker and alderman's son wouldn't be able to write convincingly of court behaviors and courtesies. The Oxfordians in England still hold to their argument.

One way to extend the background on Shakespeare would be to focus on this conflict about the authorship of the plays. I made a note for future use of that video. I thought I would divide the class in half, and have one half take notes on the evidence for the nobleman's authorship, and the other half take notes on the argument against the theory. It would be good experience before eighth grade debates.

A Readers' Theater in the Classroom

We had class sets of paperback copies of our Shakespeare plays; they were *Signet Classics* from the Penguin Publishing Company, and contained

quite accessible introductions and essays on topics pertinent to the particular play. There would be a short biography of Shakespeare, and perhaps
an essay on a famous historical production, or an actor forever connected
by name to a particular role.

As students were developing a perspective on this sixteenth- and
seventeenth-century playwright, the librarian and I worked out assigned
roles. As we read the play aloud in class, students wore an article of clothing representative of their character. One year the art teacher came to class
and showed us how to make half-masks (described in chapter 2—about
scheduling and correlating), which were especially effective for characters
who disguised themselves as others as part of the plot.

As to reading Shakespeare with thirteen-year-olds, we weren't challenging the actors at London's Globe Theater, though I did stop students
and ask how they might say their speech in today's English. Students
found the banter and the behavior of Kate and Petruchio, as well as the
flirting Bianca when she and Kate weren't involved in sibling rivalry, very
familiar. The complications of one character acting as another person to
gain access, as a tutor to Bianca, amused no end, as did the wager at the
end of Act V.

In true modern-values style, the students decided that Kate had
figured out a way to rule Petruchio while seeming to be obedient all the
time.

Thematic Good-byes

The school year was winding down. Assemblies, field trips, field day
activities, and awards programs were all changing the daily schedule and
making continuity difficult, but who can vote against celebrating the finish of another academic year? If you have to fill fragments of class periods
with no real chance of getting students to focus on being scholars, rely on
educational entertainment as a form of management. I had an entertainment source that worked to summarize all three themes we had dealt with
that year.

WonderWorks produced a two-part film in 1990 called *Sweet 15*.
It was a year or so after the amnesty period where illegal aliens could
register, be given papers to continue work, and start on the road to natu-
ralized citizenship. The film showed a comfortable middle-class Mexican-

American family in southern California planning their daughter's coming of age party, her *quinceara* (sometimes spelled *quinceañera*) that also involves a church rite for which girls do community service. In helping at the church office, the daughter discovers her father is an illegal alien who has lived in the United States for years under several false names. What better way to end the year than the portrayal of a contemporary problem where immigration, and personal frontiers, meet the land frontier where people cross into the United States illegally, and see conflicts between holding to their cultural traditions and fitting into the American culture? And isn't immigration still a question we need to face that causes conflict today?

That's exactly what we did. Students individually drafted their own understanding of how this one film represented all three themes we had studied the past year. We discussed the situation in class, and then fine-tuned their essays in case they had changed their viewpoints as the result of hearing others' reasoning. That was a tailor-made resolution to the thematic curriculum.

It was finally time to say, "Have a great summer holiday! See you next year!"

CHAPTER EIGHT
DEVELOPING GEOGRAPHY AND FRIENDS

You have read, already, so many references to things that were part of the geography theme that you may be reminded of the famous Yogi Berra quote, "It's like *deja-vu*, all over again." I will try to avoid obvious redundancy, and still give you enough information to go out and try things on your own.

Mandated Themes: Where Is the Choice in That?

The state of Virginia had a curriculum for eighth graders in social studies class: geography, government, and economics. It is possible that the sequence was also recommended, but it makes sense if you stop to think about it. Students started learning about geography somewhere along the way in elementary school: biomes in science, climate zones in social studies, all leading to a concept of what the earth was like, and where people lived.

The more people who populate an area, the more organization they need to keep order and foster cooperation. Recall the early people of the Fertile Crescent, especially in Mesopotamia, where serious agriculture had its start and led to the formation of settled town and city life. When enough food was present, people who were not needed in the fields could do other things. Learned skills might decide which persons would do what, but who was in charge?

As soon as you have organized populations, you have production, storage, and distribution challenges. Bartering and exchange only go so far, and recordkeeping and some form of exchange medium introduces the whole idea of economics. Besides, economics requires some abstract concepts most twelve- and thirteen-year-olds have not tackled to a great degree. Let them mature through two-thirds of a school year before dumping economics on them.

A Geographic Foundation

The social studies teacher, possibly helped by the science instructor, held forth on the earth, from molten core to cooling crust, which brought in plate tectonics that explained the Himalayan Mountains in Asia and the original continental mass, Pangaea. Students are impressed to see that today's South America and Africa once formed a single continent. Glaciers eventually carved out valleys and dropped huge boulders in unexpected places. Where did that leave English students?

In English and science classes, we could be literally all over the place. I, for one, am personally fond of the word itself, *geography*. There's something elegant about the thought that it means geo- (earth) and -graph (writing). Nature has written on the earth, and scientists read the story. Biomes and geology were the order of the day for scientific study, weather, and the seasons. In English class we had endless options, but we did have to read, write, speak, investigate sources, and learn grammar conventions.

The History of English

Eighth graders began with a look at a history of the English language. Students had studied immigration their previous year, and discovered where we live or have lived influences our personal lexicon. We would build on their linguistic autobiographies. This was a chance to see how Scandinavian deities gave us Wednesday, Thursday, and Friday; how the German language provided our term *kindergarten* (the children's garden); crusaders returned from the Holy Land with an Arabic word, *algebra*. We have *plaza* and *patio* from Spanish, left from the conquistadors in towns along our southern borders. We don't often use the term *piazza* in the United States, but the Italian *pizza* is everywhere.

I was surprised to learn *peach* was a combination of Persia and China, brought no doubt, along the Silk Road of Central Asia. And French derivations slipped in when William the Conqueror, from Brittany in France, won the Battle of Hastings in 1066. Suddenly French terms were elite, and Anglo-Saxon . . . well, Anglo-Saxon words still have a lower-class reputation as the result of that historical and cultural shift. Today's language shifts are more likely due to technological progress.

Technology changes jobs, and both develop jargon particular to the situations. Do not get the older generation started on computer terms and e-mail abbreviations. Just think back to the nineteenth century when the transcontinental railroad gave us the expression "the wrong side of the tracks," and the trails for herding cattle to market provided the term "watering hole." World War I's soldiers were "doughboys," whereas World War II's soldiers were GIs. Linguists say languages are always changing, which suggests that standards aren't that important. English teachers know about humorous books that firmly advocate upholding those standards.

Our students created timelines to show the historic influences on English, and the librarians steered us to slang dictionaries, which opened a new door. The Roaring Twenties had its references to "the cat's pajamas," comparable to today's "cool." Students interviewed grandparents and great-aunts and uncles, then their parents, and compared the words their forebearers used in comparable grades in school with expressions the students used in conversation. We shared the results in class.

Neologisms: Invent a Word

We had an ongoing vocabulary series, published by the Educational Testing Service of Princeton, New Jersey, that bolstered the history of English study. It was cleverly planned. Each unit had a word list taken from a certain subject or topic, such as terms involved with law and legal practices. Each lesson was introduced with an essay using the words in context, and each had a section on Greek and Roman roots. We were covering the history of English in more than one way.

Inspired by the weekly "Style Invitational" contest of the *Washington Post*, the class tackled the creation of a new word, a *neologism*. Students would invent a word for a purpose where a specific term for that situation, in their opinion, was lacking. By checking entries in the famed *Oxford English Dictionary*, and typing their efforts in that format, students shared their new words, posted on a classroom bulletin board. I have no doubt that, if families regularly gathered around a dinner table, this project inspired much shared merriment.

With the linguistic focus in full swing, a high school teacher passed something along at a fortuitous moment. It connected with the folktales from around the world that we would be reading, and also highlighted new research about language and brain activity. It had the improbable title of "Ladle Rat Rotten Hut." Just reading the words made one stop and read again.

"Ladle Rat Rotten Hut" was first published in 1956 (Chace). In searching the Internet for the source, I found a link to an article in the *Jerusalem Post* for June 14, 1996. It described a program on the Discovery Channel that reported on research showing how children as young as one year old can hear distinctions between words. That is, they could hear where individual words start and end in a spoken statement. There was a reference to the popular World War II song, "Mairzy doats and dozy doats," before the mention of "Ladle Rat Writing Hut." The article's use of the term *writing* instead of *rotten* might be questioned. Further searching found the original source.

The teacher-shared copy I received was just the ticket to give students the experience of translating into English another folktale, "Little Red Riding Hood," from what seemed like a foreign language. Here is a website with the entire contents of that 1956 publication, *Anguish Languish*, www.crockford.com/wrrrld/anguish.html. An excerpt from "Ladle Rat Rotten Hut" follows here as an example:

> Wants pawn term dare worsted ladle gull hoe lift wetter murder inner ladle cordage honor itch offer lodge, dock, florist. Disk ladle gull orphan worry putty ladle rat cluck wetter ladle rat hut, an fur disk raisin pimple colder Ladle Rat Rotten Hut.
>
> Wan moaning Ladle Rat Rotten Hut's murder colder inset. "Ladle Rat Rotten Hut, heresy ladle basking winsome burden barter an shirker cockles. Tick disk ladle basking tutor cordage offer groin-murder hoe lifts honor udder site offer florist. Shaker lake! Dun stopper laundry wrote! Dun stopper peck floors! Dun daily-doily inner florist, an yonder nor sorghum-stenches, dun stopper torque wet strainers!"

Imitating fables, the story even had a moral to underscore at the end.

MURAL: Yonder nor sorghum stenches shut ladle gulls stopper torque wet strainers (Chace 1956).

I leave it to my readers to fulfill that translation assignment on their own. Another choice would be reading the Br'er Rabbit stories in Southern dialect. They were collected and retold by anthropologist Joel Chandler Harris (1845–1908) as the stories of Uncle Remus. By now, they may have been reinstated as period literature, having fallen into disrepute during the era when we were all charged with being politically correct.

What Do You Read for a Geography Theme? True-life Adventures

In chapter 5, you saw a procedure frame (figure 5.1) that described steps in the assignment to read a true adventure book set in the great outdoors. Procedure frames spell out what and how, and help plan for when. The term for this support for students who often have trouble breaking a task into its steps is *scaffolding*. Part of the assignment was to read an excerpt from the book aloud. One student read a biography of the naturalist John Muir, for whom the California forest is named. Thor Heyerdahl's *Kon Tiki* would be another example.

A kind of biography of the earth can be found in various articles focusing on natural wonders. *The Mini Page: Especially for Kids and Their Families* is an insert in many nationally syndicated and regional Sunday papers. Recently the front page headline was "This Land Is Your Land," which probably rattles your neurons, which then begin to play, silently, the song by that name so frequently programmed in school choral concerts.

On the *Mini Page* were colored photos and short paragraph captions about Mount McKinley, Death Valley, Dry Tortugas National Park, Carlsbad Caverns, and Tallgrass Prairie. More were featured inside. What sights have your students seen at sites in the United States or even overseas? The *Mini Page* was reminding readers of Geography Awareness Week, November 16–22, 2008. Think of the creative assignments students could pursue during geography week. Celebrating this week could link science with the theme, front and center. Map the sites in the *Mini Page*, but then investigate how they happened to be there.

Representative Short Selections

A book read as part of the sixth grade survival theme was James Ramsey Ullman's *Banner in the Sky*. In the literature book, there was a short story by Ullman, "Top Man," based on his own experience with the American team that climbed the Himalayan peak known as K-2. One student observed the effect of the author's writing and how he made a character out of the mountain itself: an example of personification creating the tension in the plotline.

Along with Jack London's classic, "To Build a Fire," we had plenty of evidence of the effect of geography, and on personal response to the dangers it occasionally provided. The library had both a video biography of Jack London, as well as a print version. The video supplied a lot of information efficiently, and certainly showed us another example of how life experiences feed and influence authors' writing. We would come back to that observation repeatedly.

Stuffed away in a file drawer, I had a poem by Sarojini Naidu called "In the Bazaars of Hyderabad." The teacher's material that included it excerpted only three sections of a longer work, but the result was a pleasing and exotic view of the bazaar vendors. It appealed to the senses as it evoked vivid mental images. The entire poem is found in *A Book of Poetry—1,* from the *Perspectives in Literature* series (Enright and Marthaler 1969). The authors of the teacher's material suggest having students write a similar poem based on American supermarkets. That assignment should get creative juices going along with the salivary response.

In the poem, Naidu asked, "What do you sell, O ye merchants? Richly your wares are displayed. . . ." Or "What do you weigh, O ye vendors? Saffron and lentil and rice. . . ." And "What do you grind . . . What do you call . . . What do you cry . . . play . . . chant . . . ?" Unusual terms like turbans, brocade, amber, jade, citron, pomegranate, cither, and sandalwood evoked another culture and developed vocabulary (Enright and Marthaler 1969). If I hadn't used it in the geography theme, the vendor idea would have fit economics beautifully, too.

Also appropriate for the theme of geography was a poem by Ogden Nash, "Look What You Did, Christopher!" On the Internet, many sites provide the full text of the poem, often with comments and teaching points. For simple introductions, two children's poems are winners. Annette Wynne uses the simple title "Columbus," as does the other one by Joaquin Miller (in Arbuthnot 1952). Both poems speak to the explorer's inspiration, but also to the dangers of his voyages.

In chapter 5, we thought about teaching a concept of the essay using three examples about geography: an earthquake, a hurricane, and Columbus's voyages. Don't forget those sources.

Folktales from Around the World

Our English language history study moved nicely into reading folktales from a single language culture: a classic title for an example of these would be the South American collection, an early Newbery Medal book, *Tales of Silver Lands*, by Charles J. Finger. *The Cow-Tail Switch and Other West African Stories* by Harold Courlander and George Herzog also earned a Newbery Medal and takes students to that continent in the blink of an eye.

Despite our immigrant ancestors' bringing language and cultural diversity throughout our history, we too have tales of a language and somewhat separate culture group: that of Native Americans. Stith Thompson selected and annotated Native American stories in the collection *Tales of the North American* (1966). Libraries will provide extensive collections of worldwide folk and fairy tales, but you can't ignore *Grimm's Fairy Tales* (1972). They are famous to adults, but each and every generation must discover them anew.

Plan to use the brain's imaging system whenever possible. For the folktale collections students were reading, I asked them to notice what character types, settings, language phrases, problems, animals even, were featured in most of the stories. The challenge for them was to create something artistic, like a scene or a design that would represent the particular culture or language's tales they had read. One student created a flowing stream with lettered story titles floating by, as animals, plants, and human characters watched. What culture could that be? Did you think, "It depends upon the animals and location"?

Fiction Adventures in Geographic Settings

There is a wide range of adventures in geographic locales: *Lost in the Devil's Desert*, by Gloria Skurzynski, matches and surpasses the survival skills Sam Gribley needed in *My Side of the Mountain* simply because of the presence of death, a possibility that could occur within twenty-four hours in a waterless region. Another desert setting provides tension galore when a madman with a .356 Magnum hunts the hero in *Deathwatch*, by Rob White.

More like Sam Gribley is the character in *Hatchet*, by Gary Paulsen, who is on the way to visit his mechanical engineer father. In a small plane owned by the company working the oil fields of northern Canada, the pilot has a heart attack; Brian survives the crash and uses his only tool, a hatchet from his mother, to live in the forested wilderness. Rescue is a remote possibility. These fictional adventures were part of a three-media project.

High school students would be caught by the drama in the film *Into the Wild* (2007), which portrayed the story of Christopher McCandless, as found in Jon Krakauer's book of the same title. McCandless kept a diary of what he did and where he went as he attempted to survive in the Alaskan wilderness, but nature's challenges brought him to the film's sad ending. It is now available as a DVD.

Three-Media Projects Express Geography Different Ways

I liked to read aloud, right at the beginning of the year, from Will Hobbs's *Downriver*, where some young teens with various problems are part of an outdoor experience rafting down the Colorado River. Another classic, excerpted in a sixth grade reading series but applicable to other grade levels, is Armstrong Sperry's *Call It Courage*. The son of a Pacific Island chief is afraid of the water because as a toddler he had almost drowned. He feels ostracized, and decides to prove his courage or die in the ocean. A lot of character development occurs.

Once they had read a true adventure, a nonfiction or *true* book in a geographical setting, students picked a geographical feature like the desert, mountains, forested wilderness, rivers, seas, or islands (see figure

A MULTI-MEDIA EVENT for multiple intelligence!

What is there about a...*mountain, valley, river, ocean, beach, forest, desert, plain, hill, cliff, stream, lake, pond...*that inspires people? What can a painting show? What can music represent? How can people write about it?

Form a group of three, with a person represented from each strength area: artistic, musical, literary. "Triangulate," that is, look at a geographical feature through the "eyes" or perspectives of three media. The person with the musical gifts or interests is in charge when analyzing a piece of classical music. The analysis of a painting will be guided by the artistic "soul" in the group, and the literary-type will help the group take apart a poem or article. A summary of the group discussion and consensus of each work will be written by the person of "strength." BUT, each person will write a personal summary with individual opinions and conclusions which come from comparing the three works together.

GOAL	Week 1	Week 2	Week 3	Week 4	Week 5	Week 6
To respond to an aspect of geography	Begin reading a 150+ page fiction adventure where a writer puts characters in a situation, the outcome of which is determined by the geography of the setting.	In groups of three, begin to look for a piece of classical music, a painting or museum-quality photo, and a poem or non-fiction article all dealing with the same geographical feature you all agreed upon. Analyze the one for which you are responsible. Begin listening to the music 3 X's a week.	The "artist" should get the group together and share his/her analysis to stimulate the discussion. One person should take notes to give to the "artist" to summarize the group's feelings. Note parts and features, arrangement, color, lighting, etc. How did the painter feel about the geographical feature?	The "literary type" should share the poem or non-fiction article with the group and lead a discussion about how the author feels and what is being said about the geographical feature. A different person should take notes on the discussion so the literary leader can write the summary.	It's the musician's turn to share a personal analysis of the classical music inspired by the geographical feature, with a new person taking notes to help in the write-up of the summary of the discussion. Don't forget volume changes, speeds of passages, instruments and sections of pieces as well as hi-and low melodies or repeats. Each person writes his/her conclusion about three media communicating ideas on the same topic/thing.	Be ready to write in class about the fiction book this week. At home, respond to geographical feature with a creation of your own. You choose the medium for your own personal response. Quality and effort should be foremost.

Week Five: Remember at the end of week five, hand in the discussion-summary you wrote up as the leading "expert" in that area. As the concluding paragraph(s) to the discussion-summary, write the personal conclusions you came to as the result of analyzing the three perspectives on one geographical feature.

Figure 8.1. Procedure Frame for the Three-Media Geography Project

8.1). They needed to plan ahead because this book set the tone for a three-media project. They followed that chosen element through a piece of nonfiction, either a magazine article or a poem, in a piece of classical music inspired by the geographical feature, and in a painting or museum-quality photograph.

Remember that these themes are just that: themes. They can be developed for any class group at almost any age, by adapting projects and assignments to the students' level, or inventing completely new ones. Teachers, themselves, can take students through a three-media experience in a class period or two, or for a week's emphasis. The idea of comparing a topic from fiction, fact, music, and art perspectives works particularly well with primary grades. It is a new way of thinking. It is the novelty the brain craves.

When a class was small, twelve to fifteen students, the three-media project was an individual assignment where everyone read a geographic-fiction book along with an essay on the topic, and found appropriate music and artwork. They received a list of classical music, and I occasionally made an audiocassette copy for a student to use and return. (See appendix 3.) When the program grew, and the class reached twenty to twenty-five students, we used a small group or team approach.

The project lasted six weeks, and students considered their artistic, musical, or literary strengths before signing up to be the person responsible for that medium in the small group. I handed each student a sheet of paper that described profiles of people with the three talent areas and asked them to decide his or her own strength. I addressed the three talent areas in this handout.

Your Best Shot

We're all good at the English language—reading, understanding, appreciating, responding to, and even writing about it. It is our language. But how are you at the *aura* of any culture: at the various ways a culture expresses itself, as it interprets the world in which it exists—in other words—the arts, or as someone defined them, "the cutting edge of interpreting reality"?

Rate your strengths in three areas, relatively speaking of course. You may think you are *lousy* in all three, but even negatives are rela-

---

tive. Put a "1" by your "strong suit" as they say in the game of bridge, a "2" by your lesser talent, and a "3" by the weakest area of the three. Then hand in your personal decisions.

YOUR NAME_____

____THE ARTIST: You like to paint or sketch, to create art objects, to do folk crafts perhaps, and you even enjoy visiting art museums. You must have beautiful things around you, and put pictures up on your bedroom walls.

____THE MUSICIAN: You play a musical instrument, even take lessons and practice; you read music, listen to it on recordings and radio, and may even attend concerts and recitals of instrumental and choral works, without too much complaint. You aren't planning a career in this field, though you may be, but you can't imagine life without music.

____THE LITERARY CRITIC: You don't blanch when a book is assigned; your nose is in a book on a daily basis, what's one more? Your idea of fun is discussing what you've read with someone else. You read everything you can get ahold of, including poetry and nonfiction. You're even beginning to notice the words a writer chooses, or how she says something in an unusual way. Perhaps you've tried your hand at writing the great American novel.

The Individual Project or a Group Challenge

As an individual project, each student handed in a card with the information about the fiction book, article or poem, music, and work of art. When the effort was made by a group, members did the same thing. They not only had the procedure frame for a long-term project, but weekly reminders were posted on the assignment bulletin board.

Many teachers, even in elementary school, do not have one group all day; multiple classes are the norm. When working with three grade levels meeting in my classroom each day, I posted assignments on a bulletin board, color coded for the grade. Sixth grade assignments were in blue; those students had just arrived from elementary feeder-schools and were *cool*. The seventh grade had been around a year and were *growing* right along, so their week's assignments were in green. The eighth grade would finish middle school that year and *stop* coming to my class, so I wrote their weekly reminders in red. The reminders helped me as much as they did my students.

I always had students turn in cards by the end of the first week to be sure they had found the artwork, music, and nonfiction works inspired by their geographical feature, and all fit the goal of this project. That was especially important when there were groups of three students working together. To keep them organized, I handed them this form for recording their selections.

Geography Theme—Three-Media Presentation

Geographic Feature: _____

Poem: Title _____

    Poet _____

      Source: _____ (title)

                  _____ (author/editor)

                  _____ (city)

                  _____ (publisher)

                  _____ (copyright date)

                  _____ (page/s)

Painting: Title_____ (Date of work _____)

         Artist _____

           Source: _____ (title)

                  _____ (author/editor)

                  _____ (city)

                  _____ (publisher)

                  _____ (copyright date)

                  _____ (page/s)

Classical Music: Title_____ (Date of work _____)

      Composer _____

      Recording: _____ (CD or record title)

                  _____ (recording number)

                  _____ (recording company)

Student responsible for analysis of POEM_____

                                   PAINTING_____

                                   CLASSICAL PIECE_____

Another Way to Guide a Small Group of Students: A Memo

Guidelines are very important for helping students be effective and efficient at their work, and successful in meeting the standards of the assignments. When some students needed more specific direction, a memo such as the one that follows here did the job.

Group Presentation:
Three-Media Analysis of Geographic Feature

1. Sign up as a group of three or under the geographic feature you find most inspiring.

2. Sign for your considered strength: literary critic, musician or music lover, artistic type.

3. Locate the work you will analyze for the group: poem, painting, classical music—all of which should be classics, in that they have "stood the test of time" and are appreciated and valued by more than one generation. This is quality work.

4. Analyze the work for which you are responsible. [To my readers of this book: note the critical thinking emphasis here.]

   How did the poet, artist, or composer feel about the geographic feature?

   What are the parts and features of the poem, painting, or music?

   What does the work do, show, tell, or represent?

   By what process did the artist achieve these results?

   What message did they want to send a viewer, listener, reader?

   How effective were they? Did you get that message?

   How does this work relate to us today?

---

5. Meet with your other group members and present your analysis in a discussion to see if they react or respond in the same way. One member of the group should act as scribe and take notes about the discussion. Don't rely on your memory alone.

6. Practice what each member of the group will share with the class.

7. When your group finishes its class presentation, hand in a group report in a theme folder that includes:

  - An introduction explaining the power of the geographic feature to inspire.

  - A piece of writing from each group member, summarizing the particular work.

  - Note: Each piece of writing should conclude with the opinion of the writer as to the effectiveness of the medium to convey ideas about the geography, and a reference to the writer's personal preference for poetry, painting, or music (and why).

IF THE GROUP has a shared opinion for the effectiveness of one of the media, to divulge this, attach a concluding paragraph to balance the introductory paragraph.

Modeling the Media Study

I have led a class through a three-media experience as a classroom activity, and assigned nothing more. When groups of three students tackled the three-media project together, it was helpful to take the class through the experience as a model, or trial run. In one instance, I read aloud Will Hobbs's *Downriver*, and was fortunate to have a program from PBS-TV called "Rafting Down the Colorado" available. It represented a nonfiction article in video form, where scientists traveled on the raft and discussed the geology and historic evolution of this amazing canyon. That was quite a counterpart to the young people in Hobbs's book.

I shared some terrific photos in *The Grand Canyon: Intimate Views*, edited by Robert Euler and Frank Tikalsky (1992), and a wonderful find in Joseph Holmes's *Canyons of the Colorado* (1996). The gold mine in that collection of stunning photos was the text that had been taken from the writings of the first man to travel the full length of the river through the canyon. Civil War veteran John Wesley Powell and his crew of nine spent ninety-nine harrowing days in 1869 making that journey, a historic event.

Another video called the *Grand Canyon National Park* promised and delivered a "Spectacular Helicopter Exploration through 2 Billion Years" with classical background music, "landmarks, geological facts, figures, and theories" (1988). The background classical music selections were a bit of a distraction for me because, of course, I was going to play a recording in class of Ferde Grofé's "Grand Canyon Suite." We did both. PBS-TV offers a newer Colorado trip now.

We took the vicarious helicopter ride over the Grand Canyon, and on a different class day I listed the sections of the suite on the blackboard, but not in the composer's order. I asked the students to decide which movement they were hearing in the recording. They did very well, helped by the clip-clop of the mules during the descent into the canyon in "On the Trail." That narrowed the options.

The museum-quality artwork, which we looked at seriously, was a painting by the American artist Thomas Moran, "Cliffs of the Upper Colorado River, Wyoming Territory (1882)." It included a Native American village in the distance and a group of tribal riders heading across the painting's wide expanse to give a bit of perspective in contrast to the majestic cliffs rising behind them (Robinson 1988).

How Do You Grade Something Like This?

A comment on grading or evaluation is in order here. Based on what the procedure frame set out (refer to figure 8.1), I created evaluation sheets that were checklists of a sort. With the small groups, there were teacher *and* peer evaluation forms. I used both the student group's peer evaluations and my take on their presentation of the shared study, and combined them according to what I saw as a fair percentage.

I usually worked within a range of thirty points for various areas, feeling that a completed project of this size passed, in that it was completed and presented. Passing earned the basic seventy points for avoiding failure; then I added the results of the quality evaluation, of the actual work, to the base points for a final total. Group work can be touchy with concerned parents or responsible students who don't want to be exploited. Evaluation calls for diplomacy, and patience.

Whether the project was an individual effort or a group effort, I asked students to complete statements about their own artistic creation inspired by the chosen geographic feature. It was an instance of metacognition, and an opportunity for reflection. They completed statements like:

I chose the medium _____ because . . .
I liked the way I . . .
I think the best aspect of my creation is . . .
If I had it to do over, I would . . .

OR

One way to improve what I did is . . .

We're Going Off On A Tangent Here

We are talking about themes used with eighth graders, but a three-media combination can work with students of all ages.

If you work with children who are six or seven years old, chances are you have planned a theme on families. Without any fanfare or high-intensity spotlighting, use a folktale or story set in another country; check with the music teacher for a song from that culture; check with the librarian for some factual materials, both video and print media; and visit the art teacher for appropriate prints or sculpture. Every culture has artwork depicting families, or mothers and children. It doesn't matter if the painting is more historical than contemporary. Children know we live and dress differently than people did when our nation was first settled.

Put together sets of three or four items representing life in a different culture and then share them with the class in a kind of teacher's show-

and-tell. With older children, small groups could compare the materials you provide and tell the rest of the class about them.

For Japanese Family Day, use *The Tale of the Mandarin Ducks* (Paterson 1990). Or read aloud the picture book *Crow Boy* (Yashima 1955), about a village boy who didn't fit in with the other students because of his diminutive size. There you have the poignancy and familiar problems of being perceived as different. *The First Book of Japan* by Helen Mears (1953) is still available on the Internet, and is full of information, including an explanation of the four kinds of Japanese writing. Then it is time to bring in the arts.

The class can learn to sing *Sakura*, "The Cherry Blossom Song," in English and Japanese. The Japanese embassy might help with a resource for children on *noh* drama. And finally, there is one of a set of five colored woodcuts by eighteenth-century artist Kitagawa Utamaro called "Housecleaning at the End of the Year." The Adkins Museum in Kansas City, Missouri, displays them (Utamaro n.d.). This woodcut is a scene where four housewives are half-carrying a guest out of the house. He had fallen asleep in a corner during the previous evening's celebrations and never left the party.

The principles of rhetoric require that we consider the audience before making our choices of words and syntax. For young children more familiar with birthday parties than New Year's Eve celebrations, you can make light of this guest who must have been used to going to bed much earlier than when the party ended. For high school students with visions from online videos clips, television shows, and movies, a wild night of partying is more likely to be their reaction. In that case, change the artwork. "The Wave," a painting by Katsushika Hokusai (1760–1849), can lead a discussion in several directions with all ages of students.

Now let us return to our eighth grade theme of geography.

Writing Projects during a Geography Theme

All ages of students enjoy creating original tales in the folk style. From older students, with the chosen theme in mind, you can require that they be set in specific countries or climate regions around the globe. Students would need to use accurate details to explain cultures and superstitions, even in original writing. Later on, students may want to act out some of the best ones. That can keep them on task during short times when a formal lesson plan is difficult to accommodate, as just before a holiday break or summer vacation.

Parodies on folktales became quite the thing toward the end of the twentieth century. After a grammar lesson with "Goldilocks and the Three Bears" (chapter 5), you might share one of the books mentioned here. You need read only one, and the students will know exactly what you'll ask them to do. They may even ask, "May we try writing something like that?" Do it. Ask students to create a parody of a favorite tale they enjoyed as a *kid*. Just modernizing an old folktale can call on all sorts of creative talents.

Read through any tale from James Finn Garner's *Politically Correct Bedtime Stories* to pick one suitable for your students. *Fractured Fairy Tales*, by A. J. Jacobs, was a very popular school book club item. Popularity also blessed the author Jon Scieszka, whose books *The Frog Prince Continued* and *The True Story of the 3 Little Pigs* had even my middle school students in stitches.

Helping Your Colleagues

The social studies teacher might tell you that students have been assigned a report that will require library time, and perhaps you would like to help with this assignment. Once students are aware of how influential geography has been in developing the various ethnic and national cultures the earth's nations represent, their curiosity can be tempted. Comparisons can be very revealing.

All cultures or societies involve *individuals* born into *families* who nurture them with needed food, shelter, and clothing and begin to educate them with the mores and values of that society. Then, if they are lucky, the beginnings of *education* and training in the family can transfer to an educational system, influenced or supported by a *religion* or the *government*, and resting on an *economic* base of some kind for all citizens. There is a printable pattern called a Culture Box available at my website, madlonlaster.com.

Try just investigating the basics of food, clothing, and shelter in family life, comparing them through geographic regions; or organize a comparative study of religions, or styles of schooling. Remember the folktales of a culture or language group that were part of the reading activities? Literature is one of the arts that all societies create to interpret life to their citizens. Every society produces musical forms and instruments, graphic arts and crafts, and dramatic interpretations.

Holidays, too, are part of life in every settled part of the globe. People celebrate the milestones of life and of their history. Their religions are practiced in different ways. All of these are *cultural activities*. See them in the sorting pattern in figure 8.2. These reports can be eye-openers. What starts as curiosity can lead students to want to travel and to see for themselves. That can only make for a better future for all of us.

One social studies teacher with whom I worked for a few years found a planned unit called "Create a Continent." It served as a culminating activity that called on both skills and information students had been learning through the geography theme to that point. Once the students created the continent map on a grid, they decided on locations for five cities, and made geographical decisions based on latitude and longitude, flora and fauna.

They were continuing to write—an original explanation myth from the imagined continent's early people, an essay explaining why the cities were located where they were, and an original folktale that would demonstrate the cultural developments and values of the people on the continent. We encouraged illustrations, and the projects were displayed during the school system's Learning Fair in the spring. This project wins many a teacher's vote. It got mine.

Government and Leadership

We put away our passports and began to study the governments that might issue them. We moved into the area of political systems, and how democracy, spelled with a lowercase *d*, has been the bedrock of our nation in both pure and representative forms. While that material is a bit dry for English class, and science teachers might not be anxious to join the theme at this point (although dealing with the technology of satellites, television, and online blogging, even sites like YouTube, would be a connection), governments need informed citizens. At the sixth grade level, we did produce that school news telecast.

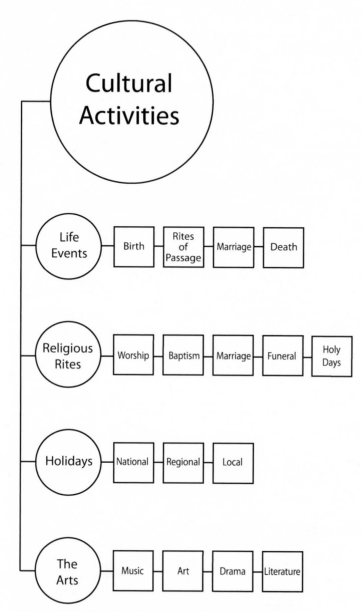

Figure 8.2. Concept Pattern for Cultural Activities

During a social studies government theme, the natural path for English teachers was to take a focus on leadership. The literary genre is, of course, biography and autobiography, which offers the benefits of discussing author techniques of characterization in the former, and character development in the latter. Depending upon the maturity of the students, teachers might introduce the elements of bias, propaganda, and reporting.

Our guidance counselor offered to hold a leadership workshop with the class (Roets 1986). But I had an option planned if she wasn't available: students would make thumbnail biographies of modern leaders at that time, the end of the twentieth century. They would cover the *who*, *what*, *when*, *where*, *why*, and *how* information. Students could pair up and use Venn diagrams to compare leaders as a way to establish basic leadership personality traits or shared qualities. Class discussion would develop a generalized description, the concept of a leader.

When the guidance counselor presented the workshop, she had enough articles to provide each student with a short piece from *Time* or *Potomac* magazines. They read them overnight and presented a brief oral summary the next day.

Seven Weeks of Leadership Topics

Week I

During the first week, we were already reading biographies of leaders across history. The library had a filmstrip set (how archaic that sounds today) that included one on the Egyptian queen, Hatshepsut, who was depicted in the stylized male profile on bas relief and tomb paintings, and who ruled with strength and more compassion than one would expect for her time. There was a good biography of Hatshepsut available—*Child of the Morning*, by Pauline Gedge. Art or history sources would lead to sculptures and tomb paintings.

Through researching and writing thumbnail biographies or via the leadership workshop, we defined what it meant to be a leader, and considered the "language of leadership," how leaders persuade people to agree with them or follow them. Toward the end of the geography theme, I had assigned the historic leader biographies our librarians had culled from the collection so we would be ready to share them in the government theme fairly early. Early turned out to be the second week.

Week 2

One of Virginia's required Standards of Learning goals was letter writing. Students worked on *persona* correspondence files at home while the speeches and panels were taking class time. They were to become the person in their biographies and prepare a file or folder with an invitation, a thank you note, a friendly letter, and a business letter that the biography character, or his or her secretary, might have written. To get into the spirit, I recommended checking the *New York City Library Desk Reference*, or an etiquette book for proper paper folds and forms.

The class would get to know their biography subjects very well as we pursued the leadership theme. Imagine a procedure frame that defines the goal and task as "To participate in a panel discussion on the topic of leadership styles." The first step warns students to be sure of the way the biography person thought, made decisions, and led other people around him or her. They were to jot notes down about when their leader did what, why, and how. The panel was another small group activity, but it involved not only adopting the persona of the biography they read for purposes of the correspondence file, but students would also portray the person in a panel discussion (see figure 8.3).

	GOAL	STEP 1	STEP 2	STEP 3	STEP 4
T A S K	To participate in a panel discussion on the topic of leadership styles.	Be sure of the way your biography person thought and made decisions, and led other people around him or her. Jot down notes about when he or she did what, why, and how.	Consider the other "people" on your panel. If you could really meet these biography persons, what would you ask them from your person's point of view? If they answered, what would you ask next?	Get together with your panel members. Ask each other your planned questions. Hear their answers. What else might you ask? Plan your answers.	Meet a second time and decide the order in which you will question each other. Will one of you moderate, or will you take turns? Add comments to fill out your "conversation."

Name	Time and Place	Area of Interest
_____	_____	_____
_____	_____	_____
_____	_____	_____
_____	_____	_____

Figure 8.3. Procedure Frame for a Panel on Philosophies of Leadership

It involved some class time for panel members to meet and plan whether they would have a moderator, take turns, or just present the conversation they might have had with each other. Questions had to be planned, and responses imagined. Remember that my inspiration for these panels was the series on PBS-TV, produced and directed by Steve Allen, called *Meeting of Minds* (Allen 1989).

An example of one of the panel discussions that took place in my classroom was one involving fourth-century Alexander the Great of Macedonia, thirteenth-century Kublai Khan of Cathay, eighteenth-century Empress Catherine the Great of Russia, and twentieth-century President Dwight D. Eisenhower. To prepare for panel presentation, each student was told to be creative in making an appropriate desk plate with name, and birth and death dates. At the time I had a reproducible page from a Good Apple publication (Cheatham 1995) in my files called "Fametoons." The names of famous people were illustrated with pertinent hints.

Robert Fulton, of steamboat fame, was printed in such a way that the *t* and *o* were in block letters, where the *t* represented a smoke stack with three clouds emanating from it. The *o* was drawn with wheel hubs to represent a water wheel. The name of the inventor of the X-ray machine, Wilhelm Roentgen, was also drawn in block letters, with bones drawn within each letter. The *Z* on Zeus was drawn as a lightning bolt. The name *Morse*, as in the Morse Code, was written with dots and dashes forming the letters' shapes. The students rose to the occasion and were suitably creative for their roles.

One year, I actually provided a checklist to be sure nothing was left undone. No one was required to wear full costume, but that could be done in other circumstances. The checklist said to prepare a five-minute speech using a standard topic outline, and to bring two copies to class. One was for the student to use, and the other was for the teacher to make notes. They were reminded that a read speech would earn a C-minus in that it wasn't a speech. The next item reminded them about the two questions they needed to have prepared from their own character's point of view.

This was the year when students would provide peer evaluations. The checklist told them they would be assigned randomly to critique a classmate's speech, including specific content information, what impressed them or they liked, what was done well, what they didn't understand, what they would like to ask, and what they would suggest for improvement in the next speech we would give in class. A friendly letter format would be used, and the teacher, of course, saw the letter first. Do not allow any feuds to start.

I have discussed the panel first here, because having an idea of the end result helps in the preparation of a more complicated process. There was a procedure frame: "To prepare to give a speech on the philosophy of leadership of a famous leader (biography)." (See figure 8.4.) The group was preparing for the panel discussions based on the speeches panel members would deliver. Did you notice that I planned the panels to include people from different periods of history, from ancient to modern? How easily you accomplish this depends on the library's collection of biographies.

We heard five panels of four and one of three members during that busy week.

There was a chapter called "The Rules of the Game" in the 1998 publication by the late scientist Carl Sagan, *Billions and Billions: Thoughts of Life and Death at the Brink of the Millennium.* Sagan discusses a set of rules symbolically identified with metals mined here on earth. The class

	GOAL	STEP 1	STEP 2	STEP 3	STEP 4
T A S K	To prepare to give a speech on the philosophy of leadership of a famous leader (biography)	Determine what leaders do or have to do to lead people: -know, -understand, -recommend, -direct, order, -judge, -plan, evaluate -ask, demand, -suggest, hint, -choose, decide, -create, etc. Check notes to see when, where and why your person lead others; see HOW it was done.	Ask yourself, "What did __?__ believe about the people s/he led? ...about himself or herself?...about what had to be done? What method(s) did they use to lead people? What would s/he say if they had to explain <u>why</u> they did what they did?	Organize your biography person's ideas about leading others. Include examples from history, from this person's life. Include explanations for his or her decisions and actions. Did the time period in which they lived affect their philosophies?	Practice giving your speech. Review the parts of a good speech from our "speech pattern" and keep them in mind as you practice. Ask someone to listen to you and time you. Keep to five minutes.

Figure 8.4. Procedure Frame for a Speech on a Philosophy of Leadership

discussion of the rules made a bridge between daily life and the way governments might function.

The Golden Rule, now considered a universal value, is offered with an interpretation, "repay evil with kindness." The Silver Rule counters with the idea of nonviolence: "Do not unto others what you would not have them do unto you." Having grown up seeing the phrase "brazen hussy!" I looked twice at the Brazen Rule, "Do as they do to you," interpreted as repaying others' kindness with kindness, but repaying evil with injustice.

Those three symbolic metals, like the three boxes of gold, silver, and lead in *The Merchant of Venice*, start an active discussion as to which serves best as a foundation for governing. But you may smile or grimace at Sagan's Iron Rule: "Do unto others as you like before they do it unto you."

The Tin Rule had three perspectives. The Bully manifestation was "Appeal to superiors and intimidate inferiors." The Kin-Selection was one I link to nepotism; the prime minister's son-in-law gets the contract despite the other bids. In favoring kin, give precedence to close relatives and treat others as you feel like it, called "Violence begets violence" by Dr. Sagan. The last perspective of the Tin Rule was "Tit for Tat," where one is to be nice on the first move, and then do whatever your opponent did the last time. That is an aspect of *game theory*. Try discussing those in English and social studies classes.

Week 3

As students were presenting leader biographies, I assigned George Orwell's allegory, *Animal Farm*, for genre, historical, and political systems reasons, to say nothing of its being a classic and the author a big name from the twentieth century. We did not view the animated film version of the book, though others might supplement the novel with the movie. In class, we were reading selections that demonstrated the heavy hand of government.

Yoshiko Uchida's story "The Bracelet" (1982), so effectively written in the first person, is set during World War II in the 1940s. It tells of a young Japanese-American girl who had a positive idea of the term *camp* and then was faced with leaving her best friend behind to go to an internment camp. Her friend's gift of a bracelet sustains her, but the poignancy and irony of the family's experience is not lost on readers, again demonstrating the power of government.

PBS-TV had a program about the Japanese internments as part of their *American Experience* series, and the timing could not have been more ideal. Students could think "I'm reading a story," when reading Uchida's description of Ruri in the camp where her family's assigned *home* was actually a horse stall. But the documentary on television was something else entirely. The story packed an emotional wallop. The television presented factual data that required an emotional reaction.

Students responded to this learning experience in writing. The first assignment mentioned the October 22, 1990, issue of *Time* as reporting, on page 35, that the U.S. Attorney General gave a presidential apology and a check in dollars to nine elderly Japanese-Americans (several over one hundred years old) in reparation. Was $20,000 each an adequate apology? In 1990 it was believed that sixty-five thousand Japanese-Americans interned during Word War II were still alive.

A second writing assignment asked students to choose between three expressions we have, and compose an essay based on their thoughts and opinions: "All's fair in love and war," "The ends justify the means," and "Circumstances alter cases." They related the chosen quote to the story "The Bracelet," wrote their essays, and then shared them in reading-response groups.

Week 4

We were finding, in publications, essays that suited our theme, and students read and discussed them in class to review our concept of what an essay is. They addressed decisions made by leaders in the past and present, and questioned what America's role should be in the world, determined mainly by the executive and legislative branches, but okayed or nixed by the judicial. One column looked at women's styles of leadership. Did they really differ from male leadership styles? We analyzed and compared to see how essays were structured and authors made their points.

Week 5 and More . . .

My colleague suggested topics on problems that came up in social studies class for which leadership was needed. These became possible individual investigation topics leading to formal research papers, and we were signed up for two periods of library time across four weeks. We researched in the traditional way with note cards, bibliography cards, outlines, and drafts with parenthetical citations, all of which required introductions in class and periodic checking on the teacher's part. We used peer-editing on rough drafts to revise before completing final research papers and later the speeches.

Week 6

PBS-TV rode in to save the day again with Bill Moyer's program, *The Democrat and the Dictator* (1984), in which he compared FDR and Adolf Hitler as men who were "masters of persuasion." We watched the program and noted the contrasts between the two World War II leaders. There was a response piece written in class, of course. Meanwhile, in grammar class, we were looking at the way clauses affect sentences and result in more sophisticated writing. I was about to introduce the idea of rhetoric, historically in Athens, and more recently with Martin Luther King Jr. These four areas would narrow in on the next step.

Armed with the results of our research, we began the persuasive speeches. Students chose an opinion they held based on the research, and planned how to persuade the class to agree with them. We had been analyzing *Animal Farm* in small groups in class, too, and used the group discussions to develop concepts that became main ideas in individual essays on that memorable book.

As soon as one book was finished, students took a deep breath, knowing another was coming. This time it was economic fiction. I wanted them to experience life in a period of economic upheaval. What better time to explore than the Great Depression, because some might still have grandparents who had lived in that decade or been raised by parents who had survived it. The economic theme was the reason for the economic fiction, yet government was involved all the way. My notes say we had a seventh week in which we wrapped up the leadership side of the government theme. Actually they overlapped. Once again, art represents life.

Week 7

To fill in some gaps and create a relaxing lull before we hit the economics theme head-on, I took the class through a three-media view of President Abraham Lincoln. *U.S. News and World Report* had a cover story on the October 5, 1992, issue with a portrait of Lincoln and the title, "Lincoln: What Made Him Great and How We Can Learn from Him" (Barone and Parshall). This was pertinent in an election year. Sections of the article included historical, mid-nineteenth-century photographs—daguerreotypes.

There was no lack of varied media on Lincoln. The class created a handout listing what we had decided about various works. One item was the painting "The Rail-Splitter," a young, ordinary, hard worker shielding his eyes from the sun, possibly looking to the future. A marble bust depicted Lincoln as an aristocrat, noble, possibly arrogant, aware of his intelligence. In various photos he always looked stern and serious, but with his son, Tad, he was fatherly. He was occasionally seen close-up as unkempt, with wild hair and coarse skin.

I'm sure we looked at a photograph of the Lincoln Memorial. The library had a videotape of "Washington, the Nation's Capital" (online, Castle Films #290), which described that statue as Lincoln sitting there and looking out over his country.

Aaron Copland's piece "A Lincoln Portrait" uses a narrator to read passages from Lincoln's statements that are inserted between passages of music. The score is melancholy and sad at times, militaristic with parade music at other times, has marches and dances, and even songs from Stephen Collins Foster, a popular composer of Lincoln's time. It worked well with the painting "Lincoln Rides through Richmond on April 5, 1865." In that scene, he was a savior who had freed the slaves, the hope of the nation, but not liked by everyone.

Trust your art teachers and librarians to help you find these. When in doubt, consult those who are expert, or at least experienced in these matters.

Another link to the Emancipation Proclamation of 1863, which freed the slaves in the slave states during the Civil War, was a popular song of that era, "We Are Coming, Father Abraham, a Hundred-Thousand Strong." My antique community songbook collection does not include this period piece. A bit of web searching turned up words, and a performance of the music, but no singers. James Sloan Gibbons wrote the lyrics, and Luther Orlando Emerson composed the music in 1862. Turn the clock back by finding period song recordings in social studies catalogues, or going to the website www.pdmusic.org/civilwar.html.

We had an array of poetry to compare via copies or the overhead projector using transparencies. Now a PowerPoint program would work beautifully for all the art and poetry. Rosemary Carr and Stephen Benét wrote the poem "Nancy Hanks," about Lincoln's mother and how proud she would be if she came back from the dead to see what her son had become. Julius Silberger wrote a "Reply to Nancy Hanks," and Nancy Bird Turner started a run of poems simply titled with Lincoln's name. Hers was just "Lincoln." Mildred Meigs wrote "Abraham Lincoln."

Carr and Benét coauthored a second poem, also called "Abraham Lincoln," a companion piece to "Nancy Hanks." They addressed his humble beginnings—being tall, strange, and uneducated, country folk, and a storyteller. Truly a classic is Walt Whitman's "O Captain, My Captain," written upon Lincoln's assassination. Its metaphor of a storm-tossed ship nearing port with its captain dead on the deck is hard to equal for demonstrating grief and regret (1951). Whitman also penned "When Lilacs Last in the Dooryard Bloom'd," about Lincoln's death, funeral procession, and the funeral train to Springfield, Illinois, a true lamentation (2001).

An article, "Reinventing Lincoln," by Sam Fink in the *New Yorker* (1994, p. 105) suggested that every generation had to reinvent Abraham Lincoln for its own point of view. Modern presidential candidates often select him as their hero. To help with that transformation, we have biographies for all ages of school students. Books abound when it comes to the life of Lincoln.

A prose selection with an index that identifies hundreds of primary sources, a book that reads like an exciting novel, is Margaret Leech's (1941) *Reveille in Washington, 1860–1865*. It describes Lincoln's arrival in Washington in disguise, how he irritated people comparing their height to his (six feet, four inches), and how a journalist described him as having "the gift of gab but it was Western gab" (p. 48). The book continues through his assassination and the nation's reaction.

Leave it to a more contemporary source to bring objective reality into the equation. In *Time* magazine for October 2, 1992, Gary Wills wrote an article, "Dishonest Abe: America's most revered politician dissembled, waffled, told racist stories and consorted with corrupt politicians—all in his noble effort to free the slaves and save the Union" (pp. 41–42). The somewhat provocative headline begins a story that recognizes Lincoln's ability to lead others to see "the great moral issues of the war" (p. 42).

Two additional comments on a theme like government and leadership: first, don't forget the cartoons and comic strips that seem to come out in newspapers and magazines at the opportune moment. That is how cartoonists make their livelihood, by responding to the news as it happens.

As Election Day approached, Hank Ketcham's long-running favorite, "Dennis the Menace," had Dennis asking how people got to be president anyway. His father decided to give an explanation by describing how a group of people tries out, and then they are narrowed down to a dozen or so; after which they are eliminated one by one, until we finally end up with two. Then we get to vote for the winner. Dennis says that he understands: "It's just like *American Idol*!" (Ketcham 2008). Which leads me to the second additional comment.

One year, an election year, I assigned nothing but presidential biographies from the present back as far as necessary to have a president for each student to study. They read their books and created the *persona* correspondence file, gave a speech on that president's leadership style or philosophy, and also planned an election campaign for their president.

The campaign package involved a radio advertisement (an audiocassette was used at that time, or performed "live"); a videotaped television campaign ad; a slogan that might be used for pins, mugs, and other memorabilia; a bumper sticker; and a magazine-page or newspaper advertisement. Picture if you will, a song and dance routine in a videotaped TV ad, adapted to the then-current pop song "My Guy."

The research papers that year were focused on an issue from that president's term or terms in office. As I read one, I learned a lot about the interstate highway plans of President Eisenhower, who had seen how the Nazi army used the German autobahns efficiently in the European Theater of World War II. They moved military transport quickly along the highways, and Eisenhower felt the United States needed a similar system, just in case.

Finally, the Economics Theme

Other than the price of bubble gum, video games, and movies, economics isn't a top priority for preteens and budding adolescents. I may sell them short with that comment, and I may be remembering a personal attitude.

How did you, my reader, feel about economics when you were in junior high or middle school?

The Question of Economics: Fiction or Fact?

It seemed wise to make a connection between the immigration theme of seventh grade and the economic theme in eighth. Upton Sinclair's *The Jungle* (1906) seemed a good choice. It exposed to public view the conditions under which immigrants labored in slaughterhouses and meatpacking plants in the Chicago area in the late nineteenth century. It roused public opinion and turned that industry around for the better, but with a great uproar from all sides at the time. It was not bedtime reading for children. But after a brief exposure to the issues, some students might read it in its entirety years later.

I read selected pages from my Penguin Classic edition (1985), starting with those that introduced the Lithuanian characters, how they looked, and where they lived. I read all of chapter 3 with its vivid description of the production line in the slaughter house. I considered another short excerpt as optional, but it did show swindling efforts to pass off bad meat through a pickling process. I watched students' facial expressions over the top of the book I held. Economics is not separate from daily life. Today, we have the Food and Drug Administration (FDA), and still occasional problems surface.

Students had begun reading fiction in an economically affected setting, and two titles are perfect examples of those books, *No Promises in the Wind* and *Out of the Dust.*

It was hard to imagine a family sitting at a meager meal during 1932 in the Great Depression and hearing the father's words about no jobs, no potatoes, and children not doing their part when they didn't find a job to help out. It was even harder still to imagine a teenager making the decision to leave home with a friend for company, to ride the rails, and to hope to find work where things were a little better. The emotional atmosphere was palpable in Irene Hunt's *No Promises in the Wind* (1993). The poor economy now, in 2008, may inspire similar literature in the future.

I chose to read aloud selected poems from Karen Hesse's *Out of the Dust* (1997), thinking that some students would be turned away by the notion of being assigned a bunch of poems in order to get the story told—even if I had shared *Spoon River Anthology* with them between the immigration and frontier themes the previous year. I read twelve or fourteen poems to sketch out the plot and make sure students realized that even some girls ran away from impossible situations. The poem "The Path of Our Sorrow" traces the cause of the Dust Bowl in history and in practice (pp. 83–84). *Out of the Dust* is quite a book.

John Rowe Townsend's *Noah's Castle* (1978) is set in a similar situation of dire straits for a family in fictional England. It demonstrates hard times in another country, which softens the blow a bit for the sensitive youngster, but not that much. As I collected the response writings to this economic fiction, we discussed the effects of economic deprivation on characters. Who managed to keep hoping, and who saw things as hopeless?

While students read, we went back to the library to research the economic period in which their books were set so they could compare the record of history with the fictional experiences the author portrayed. At this time of the academic year, it is hard to separate reading, research, and writing. Their research was used for writing an editorial that might have been printed in a newspaper of the 1930s. Then their character wrote a letter to the editor to present the character's feelings about the column.

When economic fiction books were behind them, students chose from the piles of books dealing with biographies of economic leaders that the librarians had placed on a library table. There were three or more books about the same person to make small groups easy to create, and that gave students a chance to see the difference the author's viewpoint might make on how the person was described. Students were asked to consider the following: did they worship money, were they ruthless, just lucky, was it a matter of being in the right place at the right time, or might it have been skill and know-how that let them succeed?

Groups shared the portraits or profiles of the economic leaders with the class, not exactly as a formal panel discussion, but more to bring out the differences in the writer's take on the same person.

Again we were reading articles in class from the periodicals of the time. I was providing examples of *the essay form* that made comments on society and also predictions of what present behavior and habits meant for the economic future. But we were also developing the concept of *author style* and the elements that create it.

Depending on your group of students, you might want to consider for its shock value, Jonathan Swift's "A Modest Proposal," written in 1729. It is an infamous piece of tongue-in-cheek satire with a subtitle that says, "Preventing the Children of poor People in Ireland, from being a Burden to their Parents or Country; and for making them beneficial to the Publick." Swift then describes the problem of overpopulation from high birthrates in Ireland, leading to poverty, malnutrition, and a burden on charities. Swift's horrifying solution, it is said, is offered because it will also prevent voluntary abortions. His suggestion is to eat the excess children for dinner! Economics is taken to the extreme, the unthinkable, with effect.

Reading *and* Research, the "I Search . . ." Quest

The other general reading that was assigned for the economic theme centered on "money moguls," the men who made the millions, which in today's numbers might now be worth billions. Stewart H. Holbrook's book, *The Age of the Moguls: The Story of the Robber Barons and the Great Tycoons* (1953) cited a list of such people. This was another "you and two or three others" small group study, and I asked students to keep learning logs to follow the journey in their research. Where did these moguls start? Where did they go next? What took them there?

Holbrook felt that the men fit roughly into three categories: promoters, bankers, and industrialists, which also included merchants (pp. viii–ix). He said: "The Guggenheims were both promoters and industrialists. Mellon covered the entire field. Hill, Harriman, Villard, and the first two Vanderbilts belong, as great railroad men, in a special niche. The Astors were the most successful real estate operators" (p. ix). The author talks about the men in his book (listed below) in the introduction, but the Guggenheim family includes a daughter, Barbara.

Armour, J. Ogden	Frick, Henry Clay
Astor, John Jacob	Gould, Jay
Carnegie, Andrew	Guggenheim, Barbara
Cooke, Jay	Harriman, Edward Henry
DuPont, Alfred et al.	Hearst, William Randolph
Fisk, Jim	Huntington, Collis P.
Ford, Henry	McCormick, Cyrus Hall

Mellon, Andrew   Schwab, Charles
Morgan, J. Pierpont   Vanderbilt, Commodore
Rockefeller, John D.

By the way, if you do not have time to assign full biographies, Holbrook's book has very usable chapter-length biographies of each person. Older high school students could handle the reading level and report to the class on their assigned, or chosen, mogul.

Economic Genius: "Who Has It and What Is It?" (Data summary)

- Use the resources of the library, but feel free to contact other libraries, and people who work in the same field as these economic geniuses to discover who they were/are and what made/makes them so successful?

- Keep a list of sources to present as a bibliography record of your search.

- Write your record as you go: "First we looked . . . and we found out that . . . Then we checked . . . and we learned . . . (etc.)." Try to find out:

Who: _____

Dates: Birth_____ and Death_____

Background, including family origins:

Field of economic success:

Character traits that helped with success:

Early opportunities:

Early accomplishments:

Trigger event/s? (luck or serendipity?)

Millionaire?

Techniques or rules for making a profit?

Philosophy of wealth?

Another Approach: the "I Search"

Students were given a more descriptive handout for the "I Search" assignment. It was called a Treasure Hunt for Money Moguls. Students were asked to purchase a two-column stenographer's pad, or a spiral notebook, and rule their own lines down the center of the page. They would work in teams of two, three, or independently if one's schedule were tight. They could use the library's Internet access after school if they made arrangements to stay and needed an adult chaperone. Most students today would have their own Internet access at home.

To avoid duplication, students posted the names of their chosen people on the class sign-up sheet. The directions stated:

> Select a person who is famous for his or her ability to make money. We have looked at people who lived on frontiers of knowledge or social change, who triumphed in geographical situations that meant life or death, who survived against nature or fellow humans, who excelled in leading others, who came to a new land, and not only prospered but became famous, and most recently, who conquered economic hardships. Now you want a moneymaker.

If students researched in a team, both or all had to be present at the search process. As researchers, they would keep track of the route in the left column: where they started, with what source, and what they found. In the right column, they recorded thoughts about what they found, and where they would go next. They planned a visual representation like a "road traveled," based on where they went and what they found. They created a poster they used to make a class presentation about their moneymaker.

Simultaneous Background-building

One class saw an animated preschool video created by Richard Scarry (1993) who wrote the books about animal characters who lived and worked in Busy Town. The video had the title "Richard Scarry's Best Busy People Ever." You can imagine the reaction to the announcement as class was starting that they would be watching that video. Most of the students could remember a Richard Scarry book from their toddler days. There was a hubbub of reminiscing before they settled down to watch.

This was an economic theme experience that could be appreciated by all ages and all school grades.

The video focused on how the kitten character, Huck, went with his mother or a friend to various stores, introducing the idea of producer, middleman, merchant, and customer, and dealt with career choices, as a female animal character decided to become, not an airline stewardess, but an airline pilot. These early teens were surprised, then entertained, and quickly identified the basics of economics as aimed at four- and five-year-olds. Was it propaganda for capitalism? It did bring up a discussion of fighting gender stereotyping.

Edward R. Murrow had made a milestone film on migrant workers at the end of the 1930s, called "Harvest of Shame." It was telecast on PBS-TV as part of a program on migrant workers today. It was good timing, because I was going to show the class the Henry Fonda film of John Steinbeck's *Grapes of Wrath*. I had seen a dramatized performance of this book in a theater in Wilmington, Delaware, and then the staged version was scheduled on television, too. Teachers should check copyright issues before they show a recording of a television program. I used only the film. In a drama class I would have used both the film and the staged play.

The film was a great start for noticing economic issues as involved in the plot: custom checks while crossing state lines, police discrimination, evictions, houses bulldozed, sharecroppers and tenant farmers, absentee landlords, child labor, breakup of families, strikes, oppression, poverty and hunger, migrant workers, prejudices connected with migrant workers, migrant camps, depression, people's ties to the land, the Dust Bowl, propaganda, stereotypes, and how large families had many mouths to feed. Any of these topics could be researched.

Informal Research Has a Place

Adjusting to the makeup of each class, or to a chaotic schedule, requires occasional retrenching and changing plans. A question list covered the Great Depression quickly and offered students a chance to follow their own curiosity. One year I posted the questions for students to sign up for the topic that interested them most:

Short Topics about the Great Depression to Research

1. What caused the depression of the 1930s to occur? (1929—Black Sunday and the stock market crash) _____

2. What happened when the drought caused the Dust Bowl? _____

3. How were the poor taken care of during the Great Depression? (the homeless, the unemployed, by soup kitchens, labor unions, charities?) _____

4. Why were Hoovervilles named for the president? What were President Hoover's solutions to the Great Depression? _____

5. Why did people elect Franklin Delano Roosevelt and the New Deal he promised? _____

6. What was going on in the suffrage movement? Did the depression help or hinder this progress? _____

7. Was the Hindenburg a symbol of the "Clouds of War" gathering in Europe? Explain. _____

8. What was immigration into the United States like in the 1930s? _____

9. How did radio and movies cheer people up during the depression? _____

10. How did President Calvin Coolidge fit into the picture? _____

11. Would Chicago's gangster element have developed if there hadn't been a depression? _____

12. Could the prohibition of alcohol have contributed to the Great Depression in any way? _____

13. What can we learn of the depression from painters like Thomas Hart Benton, Georgia O'Keeffe, Grant Wood, and Edward Hopper? Dorothea Lange took photographs of what she saw. Did they have more influence? _____

14. Were Martha Graham and Isadora Duncan reacting to the depression or leaders of a new movement in dance? _____

15. What inventions helped modernize life despite the economic hardships of the Great Depression? _____

16. What happened to the Jazz Age and the Harlem Renaissance when the stock market crashed? _____

17. What did Will Rogers contribute to the life of the United States during the Great Depression? _____

18. Did labor unions help or hinder the situation of employment in the depression? _____

19. What effect did the depression have on Disney Studios and other animators? _____

20. Why did communism appeal to some people in the 1930s? _____

21. Could Babe Ruth have been enough of a positive influence on baseball to carry it through the hard times of the 1930s? _____

22. Why did comics flourish in the 1930s newspapers? _____

23. What new products appeared in stores despite the depression of the 1930s? _____

24. What authors wrote fiction about life in the depression and how influential were they? _____

25. How was the automobile and its manufacturing process able to survive the economic depression of the 1930s?
_____

26. Would the depression have lasted longer if we hadn't been worried about war in Europe? _____

27. Why were fashions in the 1930s showing longer skirts for women when more fabric would raise prices of dresses and skirts at a time when a dollar a day was a wage people were glad to receive? Why had women abandoned the "flapper" look? _____

We want to keep students on their toes and learning facts while extending skills of analysis and evaluation. Spot-checks and summaries are great preparation for candidates on television game shows like the *$64,000 Question* quiz show of the past. For my students, these short question-and-answer challenges provided Great Depression background history, and food for thought in social studies class discussions. They were varied enough, topic-wise, and numerous enough to allow for student choice.

How True to Life

Some long-term projects from the social studies government theme (leadership, as pursued in English class) overlapped with economics, or at least flowed across the border. In reality we can never cleanly separate the two, so perhaps it was a symbolic solution to time pressures as the school year neared its end. We read Shakespeare before we had our debates on campaign issues. Then a video program from the Bill Moyer's series in 1984 focused on Maya Angelou, the African-American author and poet.

Watching that video as a class rounded up the year's themes nicely as we noted the effects of geography, government, and economics as they influenced society in general and Maya Angelou's life in particular. But first we had a Shakespeare play to read.

Economics Is a Large Umbrella

My intent was to read a Shakespeare play each year in seventh and eighth grades. *The Taming of the Shrew* had been an easy choice for the conflict and resolution theme in seventh grade, but what to choose for economics? That choice was no farther away than in the title of *The Merchant of Venice*. One might be a bit leery about the vitriolic speeches against Shylock, the Jewish moneylender, that students would have to read, but parents of one student suggested that a local retired rabbi, Rabbi Richman, be invited to come and speak to the class.

He was a scholar of Shakespeare and would set the attitude of the characters in the context of the times, when English law forbade usury, and some Jews were deported to Spain. My notes show Rabbi Richman mentioned Shakespeare's influence on the King James version of the Bible and on poetry, saying his works are important for their images, poetry, and human ideas, but that Shakespeare didn't understand women or black people.

The rabbi said this play was about bigotry, and the word *Jew* is mentioned in it more than fifty times. Shakespeare was in business to sell tickets and wanted to please his audience. Between 1200 and 1600 A.D. (or C.E.), there were no Jewish people residing, legally, in England. The rabbi pointed out that a play is naturally set at a certain time, and in this case, the setting was when there were no Jews legally in England. The characterization is a stereotype. He added that the play perpetuates old images of Jews, but "the play is the play." In other words, Shakespeare writes literature, not political thought.

For this play reading, students created a hat that represented the role they were taking. One of the librarians and I summarily assigned roles to students we felt could handle specific characters as well as deal with the reading of seventeenth-century English, written both in prose as well as poetry. We read the play in class as we had *The Taming of the Shrew*, stopping to translate into contemporary English, but not exactly slang. To analyze the plot and character interaction, students received a legal-length sheet of paper with story-event frames (Laster 2008) for the four main characters. These frames summarized the play.

I supplied the first and last actions of each character, and hinted at the other main actions by suggesting verbs in each frame. Each class period we would add the rest of the predicate in each frame, and watch for interactions of characters. Shylock started with "lent money at high interest rates," and ended with "agreed to sign a paper giving his daughter her inheritance." In between he "secretly planned . . . lent Antonio money . . . suggested . . . claimed . . . insisted . . . went to court . . . and won, but . . ." Who would have expected that reading the play would bring about a discussion of sentence structure and parts of speech?

While pursuing literary concepts such as characterization, interaction, and author style, we did not forget the economics theme. Using a clipping from a Sunday issue of *Parade Magazine,* where each week Lynn Minton had a column for teenagers called "Fresh Voices," I introduced the question, "What is the concept of wealth (money) in Shakespeare's Venice?"

The Minton column (1990) had asked the question, "How important is money?" Six teens ranging in age from fourteen to seventeen shared their opinions, ranging from one who couldn't imagine living without it but who saw that it could lead to fights to the Floridian who said money controls everything. Here was a natural connection for my students. I supplied the title and the setup in this assignment memo:

The Attitude toward Wealth in Shakespeare's Venice as seen in the play *The Merchant of Venice*

Recall the scenes we have read in the play script so far:

- Antonio is worried for some reason, though he claims he's not worried about his trading vessels.

- Portia is concerned that her father's will sets up a situation where she cannot use her own will (determination) to pick her husband, but has to take whoever chooses the correct casket by the way he interprets the message on the lid of the gold, the silver, or the lead box.

- Bassanio was prodigal about his "estate" (inheritance), yet wishes to borrow money from Antonio to go and court Portia of Belmont in the proper manner, and he'll certainly make enough money to repay the debt, though he might not be able to pay back what he owed Antonio from before that.

- Salanio, Solerio, Lorenzo, Gratiano, and others are bachelors and friends of Antonio who meet for dinner, fun, and conversation.

- Jessica is the daughter of Shylock who resents her father's limitations on her life in the absence of a living mother.

- Shylock festers with revenge against Christians who treat him without respect, and even revile and spit on him.

Choose your character, or a main character, and discuss his or her attitude toward wealth. Use references to the play as evidence of your reasoning. Sum up with a generalized paragraph about attitudes toward money and how this affects life and people's behavior.

This was a good time to introduce or remind students of literary allusions, too. In "And Now a Word about Sponsors . . ." Megan Rosenfeld asked, "Do Dunkin' Donuts and William Shakespeare Make a Good Team?" (*Washington Post*, May 8, 1994, p. G3). But if you can search *Time's* archives for the June 11, 1990, issue, you can roll in your own aisles with Michael Kinsley's essay, "These Foolish Things Remind Me of Diet Coke" (p. 88).

Kinsley's column is in business letter form to "Dear Sirs and Madams:" and says, "We represent the playwright, producer and screenwriter William Shakespeare in the offering of prestigious product placements in his works. . . . Billy is currently working on a docudrama about the life of King Richard III. . . . For $20,000, Bill is prepared to rewrite a line [about throwing a character in the malmsey-butt] to read, 'throw him in the super-jumbo cup of Diet Coke in the next room.'" Need I tempt you more?

In chapter 7, I mentioned a PBS-TV program on the *Frontline* series, "Who Is Shakespeare?" This would be the perfect place to use the biography, as the video argues whether a Shakespeare really lived, or did the Earl of Oxford, Edward de Vere, write the plays? On the pro side, there is proof of his existence in a signed will where Shakespeare leaves rings to actor friends, and he signs the will in three places. It is recorded in London that he owned part of the Globe Theater and owed taxes.

But for the con side, the program mentions a small book that refers to a court gentleman who is a writer but can't admit it due to his upper-class station. The Earl of Oxford wrote poetry, and was trained in the ways of nobility, which Shakespeare needed to portray in his plays, while Shakespeare was just a glove maker's son raised in a small town. Viewing this video for pros and cons requires thought, note-taking, and holding to a perspective, a good lead-up to debates.

Other Writing Experiences

An assignment sheet for *The Merchant of Venice* begins with the direction, "Design and wear a hat appropriate to your role." It continues: "While reading, watch for a set of 25–35 lines that would be interesting to translate into contemporary idiomatic English. Choose a monologue and do the translation by yourself; or choose a conversation between two characters, in which case, work with another person to translate the dialogue and be ready to read it to the class."

One year, choices were not left to chance for the translation. A list of eight recommended excerpts was provided with the assignment:

1. Portia and Nerissa from act I, scene 2, lines 1–52.

2. Gratiano, in act I, scene 1, lines 80–104.

3. Portia and Nerissa, continuing act I, scene 2, lines 53–120.

4. Gratiano, Salerio, Jessica, and Lorenzo in act II, scene 6, lines 1–68. (Borrow someone to be Antonio when you present your version in class.)

5. Jessica and Lorenzo in act V, scene 1, lines 1–48.

6. Bassanio, Nerissa, Gratiano, and Portia in act V, scene 1, lines 128–93.

7. The Duke and Shylock in act IV, scene 1, lines 16–62.

8. Portia and Bassanio in act V, scene 1, lines 192–223.

Do acquaint yourself with a book that describes doing Shakespeare with fifth and sixth graders (Cullum 1968). It will open up a whole new aspect of living with the Bard, Shakespeare, worthy of tackling. Other sources for working on Shakespeare plays with younger children as well as high school students is our friendly pbs.org, where teaching aids are available, even a specific reference to thematic teaching.

Back to the assignment.

The third item in the list of assignments is a reference to the essay on the attitude toward wealth in the play. But item four tells students to form a group of four people, and if possible, go to a business or organization in town and ask for a job application, or use the general application the teacher would supply. Checking with the teacher was a way to make sure no other group was duplicating their character choice.

The directions continued: "Decide what career your character would follow if living today. Fill out the application, and include two letters of recommendation with each resume and application. Invent appropriate information, but where character references are concerned, refer to evidence from the play and authenticate with parenthetical citations for act, scene, lines."

Lest all of you reading this book are rolling your eyes and thinking your students could not tackle some of these activities, think again. Depending on the age of the student, could they consider which character would be a good babysitter, who would be an errand boy for an office or bank building, who would be the kid in class from whom everyone else borrowed money because he always seemed to have a lot, who runs a lemonade stand each summer, or charges his parents for his time helping them with computers?

If you have time to fit in another assignment, have fun one day writing "Classified Ads for *Merchant of Venice* roles in *The Venetian Gazette*:

Who should apply for this position?" I have a filed copy advertising "Wanted: Christian woman of youthful appearance, obedient to orders, to accompany master as torchbearer, call 555-5516." I have no other reference to this creative writing challenge in my files collected from over the years. There is only an ordinary-looking page divided into columns, with the title: Who should apply for this position? The columns have brief job offerings.

During another year, students wrote classified ads when I told them to "Let your memory of the play and of the characters try to match roles with these job offers: adult escort, model, supporting actress to play pants role, financial advisor, activity planner, bartender, moneylender, sailor, translator." Students used their imaginations in the writing of the personal ads, like the one describing a tall, blond, female nonsmoker, and the want ads looking for a "ruthless, wily accountant," a nurse, or a clown.

The activities above deal with characterization and character development by applying the play's information to experiences in daily life, such as applying for jobs and answering classified ads for jobs you think sound right for you. They provided a little levity. We were dealing with the end of a year of serious reading on our various themes. Shakespeare was also the *grand finale* for checking the concept of author style. I used a sheet of typing paper ruled into three rows of three boxes each: nine elements to look for in author style.

You might want to grab a piece of scrap paper, right now, and draw a wide rectangle that you divide into three rows with two horizontal lines, and with two vertical lines, you create three boxes in each row. Across the top row, the three boxes should be labeled *Narration*, *Theme*, and *Syntax*. In the middle row, the three boxes should be labeled *Setting*, *Allusions*, and *Diction*. The bottom row of three should be labeled *Symbols*, *Tone*, and *Characterization*. Your nine boxes are now ready to go.

When it came to the element of *Narration* (first box, top row, left), we decided that characters acted out the parts, and used aside speeches. For the *Theme*, we decided *The Merchant of Venice* emphasized trust and love, hate and betrayal. *Syntax* considered word order. "I know you not" was an example we filled in, and also the stilted sentence, "Wear you yet the habit of a lawyer?"

Slip down to the middle row. *Setting* was easy to pinpoint with sixteenth-century Venice and environs. As to *Allusions*, we had noticed Biblical references to Laban, Lot, and their sheep, also Barabbas; and there were the mythological characters of Troilus, Cressida, Thisbe, Phoebus, and Dido. *Diction* represented word choice. Shakespeare emphasized gentleman as a man of gentle birth. Instead of nice, a man might be fastidious. Odd spellings existed, like *moe* for *more*. Virginia students heard that as dialect and were most amused.

The bottom row began with *Symbols*: gold, silver, lead caskets rated high in this category, but so did rings for love and loyalty, and we can't overlook the "pound of flesh," surely symbolizing life. *Tone* can be an elusive term, but tell students to think of their tone of voice depending upon the mood they are in at the moment. We have all experienced mothers who have said, "Don't use that tone of voice with me, young lady!" For *Tone*, we decided Shylock was sarcastic, cynical, nasty; Nerissa was confident, and assertive. The Prince of Morocco was frustrated, and the tone of the ring episode between the lovers was humorous.

The last box, *Characterization*, is a concept that teachers work on from the time students begin reading in what we now refer to as chapter books. Shakespeare used stereotypes: Jewish Shylock, a clever woman tricking her husband, honorable friends, bumbling clowns. For comparison, I shared a page or two from the work of another writer, Thomas Kyd, also a sixteenth-century playwright. Kyd was born six years before Christopher Marlowe and Shakespeare, and died at the age of thirty-six in 1594. We were all surprised to see characters with names like Balthazar, Horatio, and Lorenzo in *The Spanish Tragedy*.

A plus from this source (Kyd 1987) was a drawing of an open-air Elizabethan theater on the cover of the edition edited by J. R. Mulryne. Shakespeare can appeal to all ages and stages, and he was just one of several famous playwrights of his time.

Extending Shakespeare with Technology

Let me complete this section on Shakespeare's *Merchant of Venice* by encouraging you to look for sources like old television programs that *educational channels*, as they used to be called, might have in their libraries. The Illinois Shakespeare Festival stages plays outdoors in the summer daylight hours, much as I remember happened with Shakespeare in New York City's Central Park. The director of the Illinois festival created a series of fifteen-minute programs, *Shakespeare on Stage*, dealing with selected plays. *Othello*, *Macbeth*, and *The Taming of the Shrew* are three in the series, but there were others.

Each play was treated in three or four fifteen-minute programs dealing with language, setting, and characters. They were a wonderful introduction, especially to *The Taming of the Shrew*, which was read in seventh grade, because this production was set in the sombrero-style, old Southwestern culture. That in itself was an idea most students didn't know about—setting the sacred scripts of Shakespeare in other times and places. While programs on *The Merchant of Venice* weren't available then, the program on language supplied with the set on *Macbeth* was very helpful. Illinois State University and the Illinois State Shakespeare Festival produced the series in 1983, in Normal, Illinois.

A staff person at WVPT wrote me that the series is still telecast on its channel because it had bought a license that permits continuing use. I thought if the films were no longer available, other visual aids have surely taken their place.

Another Year Closes

A school year comes to an end. The year sounds so full that one wonders how we did it all. But that is just it: we didn't do everything every year. The chapter mentions little or nothing of eighth grade grammar, which took us through dependent clauses as nouns, adjectives, or adverbs, and also through verb conjugation, and *verbals*—participles, gerunds, and infinitives. Grammar was the same each academic year; the rest was up for choosing. Teachers keep collecting learning activities and strategies for all of their professional lives, whether they use them every year or not. Think of their file cabinets, bookshelves, and computer databases.

I think of the African proverb: "When an old person dies, the village loses a library."

EPILOGUE
LAST THOUGHTS

Images keep circulating through my mind, bidden and unbidden, as I sit at my computer writing these pages, and so I remembered a project students loved so much that they even enlisted peers in their neighborhood to pull it off. Yet I never mentioned it in the chapter about the five themes for the sixth grade. The school news television program was part of the original five themes. These newscasts came up a decade later.

Just as Steve Allen's series called *Meeting of Minds* inspired panel discussions on leadership philosophy, mixing Julius Caesar with FDR or Catherine the Great of Russia, I had a "Why not?" reaction to a University of Texas's 1984 series titled *Newscast from the Past*. It was also produced for PBS-TV. Finding references to cite for readers' use was an almost futile effort. I did find the name of the history consultant on the website for the university, Janet Meisel (1984).

I am unbelievably happy to tell you that you can find the PBS series *Timeline*, produced by PBS-Maryland, as well as *Newscast from the Past* available as DVDs from the middle school catalogue offered at www.socialstudies.com. I call them fabulous finds. They have great value for simply viewing in social studies class, and can be a springboard to student-produced newscasts of historic events too.

One year, when the sixth grade social studies chapter brought up the Italian Renaissance, the timing coincided with the scheduled airing of *Newscast from the Past* on the public television channel (WVPT) from Harrisonburg, Virginia. The most vivid picture in my memory is of an Asian-American news reporter in period dress and appropriate environs reporting on the death, that day, of Leonardo da Vinci. It was just like the segments on news programs today whenever anyone famous dies.

Because of their pertinence, the class watched that *Newscast* and other episodes that fit our studies. But when the textbook chapters on World War I and World War II approached, and the school year was signaling the wind-down, we needed to be thorough and efficient with our lesson time. I thought the format of a video program set in the past, when television didn't exist as it does today, would be just the ticket. We had exploited newspapers the same way.

Students loved wielding video cameras and crawling up and down banks in backyards, wearing soldiers' helmets. They worked out costumes, sound effects, and interviews with famous people or folks on the street, just as in prime-time news programs. They had to find more information than the social studies text provided, make informed decisions on what to include, and how best to fit it into the telecast. They became experts. When the rest of the class watched the video, it was unforgettable. With today's cameras embedded in cell phones and with small digital cameras taking videos, telecasts would be much easier to replicate.

Computer-Enhanced Photos

Keep asking yourself, "To what end can I ask students to use the information, the content of this topic, as part of the overall theme?" The first time I ran into computer-edited photographs of animals circulating in an e-mail, I contacted my former science and math teacher colleague, not yet retired. Had he seen these, and what did he think? On February 29, 2008, I received this e-mail:

> I saw the cloning pictures. What a stitch. I haven't done much photo-edit, however . . . we "photo edited" a head shot of . . . [the guidance counselor]. . . .
>
> Think of this: you're getting close to the end of the week; probably Friday afternoon or just before a vacation and the kids in the class are mind wandering. You break them into groups, give them a picture. They classify it (down to genus: species): give it a name; habitat; eating habits; behaviors; hunting habits; place in the food chain/web with justification; and even, effects on the food web when the 'evolution' occurred . . . etc.

I bet they could come up with some funny stuff BUT they would have to follow classification/habitat rules, so it doesn't become a free for all, but [Oh my goodness, what a concept] a fun application of learning (GCC).

Keep These in the Back of Your Mind

Activities generally fit into categories, like constructions and models; illustrations and graphics; oral presentations, such as acting out, dramatizing, or imitating as in simulations; writing in various forms; and reading.

When you decide the best media for learning the information for each theme—via reading, for example—you can think about the range available: literary groups focusing on a novel, individual reading assignments (using or not using procedure frames), articles, excerpts, poetry, biography and autobiography, comics and cartoons, how-to directions, forms and applications, notes and memoranda.

Consider oral presentations where language is used as the medium of exchange. You can choose from debate; speech (expository, persuasive, personal); dramatics (script reading, reading aloud [forensics], skits, one-acts, scenes, whole plays); panels; and reporting. If writing is appropriate, however, will it be researched or creative, and in what form?

I know there was my alphabet mind-dump list of projects in an earlier chapter, and I referred you to Don Treffinger's ABCs of projects (1989) in appendix 2. I just can't leave the topic of theme-teaching without mentioning projects again in summary. I know not everyone reads prefaces and epilogues unless they are very curious about what they will find there. I hope you are still looking for more ideas, and I know the project approach is my favorite sermon topic: we learn when we are involved.

Remember the Rationale

Some things about thematic teaching cannot be stressed enough. Themes aren't just ways to entertain and keep students busy and out of trouble. They help the mind organize related thoughts, information, and experiences.

Choose your themes carefully rather than frivolously. A unit on the circus might be just the trick for young children, but how will it serve them academically? You might have to author some story problems for math class along a plotline about a trapeze-artist family. There are generations of circus families. Poems and stories abound. Circuses were outlets for frustration in the depression. Just don't give up too soon. Be sure to make it worthwhile. The extra effort it takes to create some needed activities in the beginning builds up a repertoire from which to choose later.

Assignments that require gathering and manipulating information to create the product will yield the greatest results in mental networking, understanding, and retention. Students don't just remember the fun they had; they remember the *stuff*, the information they had to organize. I used to worry that students would remember being actively involved with friends in the thematic simulations and wouldn't remember the content information. Brain research tells us that learning in social situations *takes* better.

Basically, you think of connections between subject areas, disciplines of knowledge, based on your own education and experience, or based on group-think if a team of teachers is cooperating. In English, you want students, each week, to read (fiction, nonfiction, poetry) and write (creative, responsive, expository), discuss and report orally in the class or with smaller groupings, and get to the library for specialized resources during one class period or another.

English teachers need to schedule grammar regularly because on a daily basis we can all see in print formats, and even listening to presidential candidates, some jarring problems. Hear how nominative pronouns are replacing objective pronouns when two personal pronouns follow a preposition as *between* or *to*. Those writing workshop minilessons didn't make a difference after all. To communicate clearly, it is still important to learn correct Standard English.

When students are invested in their learning experiences and expecting to transfer ideas beyond one content area, the potential for long-term learning increases:

In the continuum of life, the cumulative (past) experiences of early childhood form the bases for children's outcomes by the time children enter kindergarten or primary school (by age 8, or ages 5–7), and these outcomes set trajectories for children's health, learning, and behavior throughout adolescence, adulthood, and later life. This conceptual continuum—from early experience to early child development to human development—is borne out by new knowledge from the neurosciences, biological science, psychology, health sciences, economics, social sciences and education . . . the effects of early experience on the wiring and sculpting of the brain's billions of neurons last a lifetime (McCain and Mustard 2007, p. 255).

And One Last Plea

Consider the characteristics students will need in the future. Working with themes, especially the variety of activities that include individual, group, reflective or public, written or oral, prepares them with a range of experiences and skills that cannot help but develop adaptive personalities. The themes discussed in this book are listed in appendix 4 by the chapters where they are mentioned or discussed.

> The global workplace favors individuals who have intellectual flexibility, problem-solving skills, emotional resilience, and capacity to work with others in a continually changing and highly competitive economic environment. The need to maximize human potential has never been greater. Countries around the world now have a special opportunity to promote the full development of their children by drawing on scientific evidence concerning child development. . . . Some may say that this opportunity is a requirement—because countries must invest in their children now if they want to be full partners in the fast-emerging global marketplace (Young and Richardson 2007, pp. 287–88).

See You in Cyberspace

Your teaching generation has tools mine didn't even know enough to dream about when taking education courses for our own career preparation. I have heard "When in doubt . . ." used to start various admonitions all my life. My mother cautioned, "When in doubt, do nothing," which was an early warning sign for situation ethics, I'm sure. Then one of the domestic humorists of the last century, either Peg Bracken or Erma Bombeck, said, "When in doubt, throw it out," referring to refrigerated leftovers of course. Let us add another dictum: When in doubt . . . search.

Currently, if teachers are too busy to sit in the lounge and chat with other teachers about what they are doing, they can just stay up late after their papers are graded and surf the web. Use one of these search phrases, "expeditionary learning" or "thematic teaching," and you'll find a lot of options. By going directly to the websites thinkingmaps.com or edutopia .org you may even forget to go to bed. Perhaps the best skill we can teach today's students is how to choose well.

Bless you all for being teachers, aspiring teachers, parents, home-schooling parents, principals, and supervisors, educators of all sorts working for the good of our children.

MTL
Fall 2008

EIGHTH GRADE
THEMES AND ACTIVITIES CHART

8	LITERATURE	WRITING *(adv. vocab units 1-17)*
G E O G R A P H Y	*[Concepts of Setting and Characterization]* "Top Man"-Uhlman "To Build A Fire"-London Geographic Fiction World Folk Tales	Influences on personal language Poem-setting of geog. fiction Character Essay OED style entry for "original word" Translation of "Ladle Rat Rotten Hut" Language-Essay Folktale Parody Hallowe'en Story Learning Logs 6-week project on Geog. Theme fiction-poem/essay-music-art
G O V E R N M E N T	*[Concept of Short Story Concept of Novel]* "The Bracelet"-Uchida Animal Farm-Orwell Biography of a "Leader" Alternative- US President	Group Analysis <u>Animal Farm</u> and collaborative essay with guided revision Persona Correspondence from Leader Biography. Paper on Topic Chosen for independent investigation -formal style with citations. FDR/Hitler Video-Response contrasting leadership styles WWII Leaders-Essay in Response
E C O N O M I C S	*[Concept of Author's Style]* Econ.-setting fiction Economic Leader's Biography "Merchant of Venice"-Shakespeare Intro. to play and selected articles	Hugh Sidey essay analysis Norman Cousins essay response D.C. Field Trip "writing" piece Econ. Fiction Setting Essay Shakespeare play analysis Monologue translated into contemporary vernacular Character description of selected role and reference to contemporary personality Concept of wealth in Shakespeare Response to Shakespeare's "style" (Merchant)

Figure A.1   Eighth Grade Chart of Themes and Activities (Appendix)

170

LIBRARY USE	SPEECH	GRAMMAR
Timeline of History and Influences on English Language	Oral reading of excerpt from true geographical novel Presentation of analysis: folktale comparison "Tell a Horror Story" (read aloud original piece)	Subjects and Predicates Review Parts of Speech Clause Patterns w/ Complements Basic Clause Patterns Subordinate clauses, concept of
Research in Library for independent investigation topic (formal paper) Could be an issue from campaign for President	Leadership Workshop w Character Traits Survey Speech-expository: Philosophy of leadership for biography person Panel Participation: Represent biog. character Election Campaign	Generative sentences Clauses: adverb, adjective, noun Diagramming for types of clauses
Research for Debate Propositions with Team Research on setting for econ. fiction, historical causes and facts.	Reading roles in class from "Merchant of Venice" Persuasive Speeches (topic from individual investigation paper) Group discussion/ presentation for class econ-leader biography Debates on topics growing out of research and speeches.	Verbals: participles, gerunds, infinitives Concept of Conjugation of Verb: person, tense, voice, mood

ABCs OF STUDENT PROJECTS

A
Advertisement
Advice column
Album
Allegory
Ammonia imprint
Anagram
Anecdote
Animation
Annotated bibliography
Announcement
Anthem
Apparatus
Aquarium
Artifacts
Associations
Audiotapes
Autobiography
Axiom

B
Baked goods
Ballet
Banner
Batik
Beverage
Bibliography
Billboard
Biography
Book
Box
Brochure
Building
Bulletin board
Business

C
Cartoons
Calendar
Campaign
Case history
Case study
Catalogue
Ceramics
Charts
Checklists
Clothing
Club

Collage
Collection
Comedy
Comic book
Community action/service
Compound
Computer program
Conference
Conference presentation
Convention
Costume
Course of study
Crossword

D
Dance
Debate
Demonstration
Design
Diagram
Diorama
Directory
Discovery
Display
Drama
Drawing

E
Editorial
Energy-saving device/plan
Equipment
Estimate
Etching
Eulogies
Experiment

F
Fabrics
Fantasy/science fiction
Feature story
Film
Filmstrip
Fiction
Flags
Flannel boards
Food
Formulas
Furniture
Future scenarios

G
Gadgets
Gallery
Game
Garment
Gauge
Gift
Glass cutting
Graph
Graphics
Greeting cards

H
Handbills
Handbook
Hatchery
Hats
Headlines
"Helper" service
Hieroglyphics
Histories
Hologram
"Hotline"

I

Icons
Ideas
Identification charts (e.g.,
"Know Your Fish")
Images
Index
Inscription
Insignia
Instrument
Interviews
Inventions

J

Jamboree
Jazz
Jewelry
Jigsaw puzzle
Jobs
Joke, joke book
Justification
Journal (personal)
Journal article

K

Kaleidoscope
Keepsake
Kit
Knitting

L

Labels
Laboratory
Ladder of ideas
Languages
Latch hooking

Laws
Layouts
Learning centers
Leatherwork
Lei
Lesson
Letter to editor
Library
List
Lithograph
Log
Looking glass
Lounge
Lyrics

M

Machine
Macramé
Magazine
Magic trick
Map
Marquee
Masks
Meetings
Menu
Meter
Mobile
Model
Monument
Mnemonic device
Mural
Museum

N–O

Newsletter
Newspaper

Newspaper ad
News story
Notice
Novel
Oath
Observance
Observatory
Observation record
Occupation
Opera
Opinion
Oration
Orchestration
Organization
Origami
Outline

P

Painting
Pamphlet
Papier mâché
Parodies
Patterns
Pennants
Petition
Photograph
Pillow
Plan
Poem
Poster
Prediction
Press release/conference
Production (show)
Prototype
Puppet
Puppet show
Puzzle

Q–R

Quarterly report
Query
Question
Questionnaire
Quilling
Quilt
Quiz
Radio program
Rating
Reaction
Recipe
Research report
Resolution
Review
Riddle
Robot
Role-playing

S

Satire
Scrapbook
Sculpture
Set/scenery
Short story
Silk screen
Simulations
Skit
Slide show
Slogan
Song
Speech
Stained glass
Steps
Store
String art

Stuffed animal
Survey

T–U–V
Tape recording
Taxonomy
Television
Term paper
Terrarium
Test
Theme
Theory
Tie-dyeing
Tool
Tour
Toy
Transparencies
Travelogue
Uniform
Unit of study
Vehicle
Verse
Videotape
Vignette
Visual aid
Volume
Volunteer program

W–X–Y–Z
Walking tour
Wall hanging
Weather map
Weaving
Whittling
Wire sculpture
Woodcarving
Woodwork
Word games
Written drama
Xerographic print, collage
Xylographics
Yardstick
Yarn (story/fabric)
Yearbook
Yodel
Yo-yo
Zigzag
Zodiac
Zones
Zoographic studies
Zoological projects
(D. Treffinger 1988)

A SAMPLING OF CLASSICAL MUSIC INSPIRED BY GEOGRAPHIC LOCATIONS

Composer	Title	Region
MOUNTAINS		
Copland, Aaron	*Appalachian Spring*	Appalachia
D'Indy, Vincent	*Summer Day on the Mountain*	France
Hovhaness, Alan	*Mt. St. Helen's Symphony #50, Op. 360*	USA West
Mussorgsky, Modeste	*A Night on Bald Mountain*	"Russia"
Strauss, Richard	*Alpensymphonie*	Austria/Switzerland
PLAINS		
Balakirev, Mily	*In Central Asia*	Central Asia
Balakirev, Mily	*Islamey*	Central Asia
Borodin, Alexander	*The Steppes of Central Asia*	Central Asia
Copland, Aaron	*Billy the Kid, Part II, Prairie*	USA
MEADOWS		
Beethoven, Ludvig von	*Pastorale Symphony (#6)*	
RIVERS		
Debussy, Claude	*The Petite Suite, En Bateau*	France
Grofé, Ferde	*The Mississippi Suite*	USA
Smetana, Bedrich	*The Moldau*	Bohemia, Czechoslovakia
Thomson, Virgil	*The Mississippi Suite*	USA
OCEAN/SEAS		
Debussy, Claude	*La Mer*	
McLaughlin, John	*Concerto for guitar and orchestra, The Mediterranean*	
Mendelssohn, Felix	*Calm Sea and Prosperous Voyage*	
Vaughn-Williams, Ralph	*Symphony #1, The Sea*	Europe
Vivaldi, Antonio	*La Tempesta di Mare (Storm at Sea)*	

SKIES/SPACE

Delius, Frederick	Song Before Sunrise	
Milhaud, Darius	The Creation of the World	
Holst, Gustav	The Planets (recommended: "Jupiter")	Southeast USA

SPECIFIC PLACES

Albeniz, Isaac	Iberia	Spain
Copland, Aaron	El Salon Mexico	Mexico
Chabrier, Emmanuel	España	Spain
Chavez, Carlos	Sinfonia India	India
DeFalle, Manuel	Nights in the Gardens of Spain	Spain
Debussy, Claude	Iberia	Spain
Delius, Frederick	Florida Suite	Southeast USA
Gershwin, George	An American in Paris	Paris, France
Holst, Gustav	Somerset Rhapsody	England
Lalo, Edouard	Symphonie Espagnole	Spain
Respighi, Ottorino	The Pines and Fountains of Rome	Rome, Italy
Vaughn-Williams, Ralph	Norfolk Rhapsody	England

THEMES DISCUSSED IN THE BOOK

Chapter 1—You Don't Have to Go Whole Hog at the Beginning

Ancient Greece and Rome, mythology, and constellations
Geography: mountains, rocks, Indian lore
Japanese mystery book: setting, song, origami
Expanding communities
Palindromes in math and English

Chapter 2—Coordinate and Correlate: Schedule and Share

Correlating cuisines with global cultures
Reference to Greece, myths, universe
Television study
Middle Ages
Conflict and resolution theme and Shakespeare's *The Taming of the Shrew*
Owl pellets and archaeology
Developing themes of immigration, frontiers, conflict and resolution, also geography, government, and economics
Reference to Ellis Island simulation

Chapter 3—Integrating Interdisciplinary Approaches

Reference to Greece and myths
Five themes of geography study
Geography as a theme

Chapter 4—Social Studies Can Rule the Day: Themes to Lesson Plans

Energy as a possible theme
General Topics of Concentric Circles curriculum for sixth grade:
Survival
Answers: Mythology and Astronomy
Scientific Law and Order
TV: Communicating through Energy
Forces: Ecology and Environment—includes activities: overnight
field trip, Cave Man Day in the Park, TV study and telecast

Chapter 5—Theme-based Learning Activities

Reading references for geography and government themes
Grammar connections to geography and frontiers themes, with
examples

Chapter 6—Simulations: Do-It-Yourself and Ready-Made

Middle Ages
Reference to *Galaxy* from Interact of California (1980)
Christendom, *Ecopolis*, *Gateway*, *The Transcontinental Railroad*,
The Donner Party, and *The Romans* from the websites that
continue to carry Interact of California products

Chapter 7—Some Successful Examples from the Past

Getting to Know You activities
Themes described: immigration, frontiers, conflict and resolution

Chapter 8—Developing Geography and Friends

The history of the English language
Neologisms
Geography, government (leadership), and economics themes

Epilogue—Last Thoughts

Newscast from the Past
Cloning pictures with photo-edit features
Reminders and websites

REFERENCES

Allen, Steve. 1989. *Meeting of Minds: First Series*. Amherst, NY: Prometheus Books.

Altman, Alex. 2008. "A Brief History Of: Summer Vacation." *Time*, June 20, p. 18.

Arbuthnot, May Hill. 1952. *The Arbuthnot Anthology of Children's Literature*. New York: Scott, Foresman and Company.

Barnes, Peter, and Cheryl Barnes. 1996. *House Mouse, Senate Mouse: How Our Laws Are Made*. Laurel, MD: VSP Books.

———. 1998. *Marshall, the Courthouse Mouse: A Tail of the U.S. Supreme Court*. Laurel, MD: VSP Books.

———. 1998. *Woodrow, the White House Mouse*. Laurel, MD: VSP Books.

Barone, Michael, and Gerald Parshall. 1992. "Who Was Lincoln?" *U. S. News and World Report*, October 5, pp. 70–77.

Berlin, Irving. n.d. "Give Me Your Tired, Your Poor" (song). Recorded on *Fred Waring and the Pennsylvanians in Hi-Fi*. Los Angeles: Capitol Records, W845.

Blackwell, Lucia. 2008. "Student Testing Program Stresses Many; No Big Deal for Others." *News Journal*, Wilmington, DE, March 10, p. E-3.

Bluth, Don. 1986. *An American Tail* (animated film). Los Angeles: Universal City Studios.

Bock, Jerry, Sheldon Harnick, and Joseph Stein. 1964/1971. *Fiddler on the Roof: The Broadway Musical* (film). New York: United Artists.

Bruner, Jerome. 1962. *The Process of Education*. Cambridge, MA: Harvard University Press.

REFERENCES

Caduto, Michael J., and Joseph Bruchac. 1988. *Keepers of the Earth: Native American Stories and Environmental Activities for Children*. Golden, CO: Fulcrum, Inc.

Carr, Rosemary, and Stephen Vincent Benét. 1952. "Abraham Lincoln, 1809–1865." In *Time for Poetry: The Arbuthnot Anthology of Children's Literature*, Book 1. New York: Scott, Foresman and Company.

———. 1952. "Nancy Hanks, 1784–1818." In *Time for Poetry: The Arbuthnot Anthology of Children's Literature*, Book 1. New York: Scott, Foresman and Company.

Cather, Willa. 1976. *My Ántonia*. Boston: Houghton-Mifflin Company.

Chace, Howard L. 1956. "Ladle Rat Rotten Hut." *Anguish Languish*. Englewood Cliffs, NJ: Prentice-Hall.

Cheatham, Val R. 1995. "Fametoons." In *Challenge*, Good Apple issue 67. New York: McGraw Hill.

Courlander, Harold, and George Herzog. 1986. *The Cow-Tail Switch and other West African Stories*. New York: Henry Holt and Company.

Craig, George C., III, and Madlon Laster. 1984. *Concentric Circle: An Interdisciplinary Program in Science and Language Arts*. Unpublished manuscript.

Cullum, Albert. 1968. *Shake Hands with Shakespeare*. New York: Scholastic.

Culp, Elizabeth Price. 1982. *Keys to Good Language* (graded workbook series). New York: Phoenix Learning Resources.

Dale, Edgar. 1946. *Audio-Visual Methods in Teaching*. New York: The Dryden Press.

Dana, Barbara. 1986. *Necessary Parties*. New York: Harper and Row.

de Angeli, Marguerite. 1949. *The Door in the Wall*. New York: Scholastic.

Debnam, Betty. 2008. "This Land Is Your Land." *Mini Page* insert, *Washington Post*, November 9.

DeVoto, Bernard, ed. 1971. *The Portable Mark Twain*. New York: The Viking Press.

Euler, Robert C., and Frank Tikalsky. 1992. *The Grand Canyon: Intimate Views*. Tucson: University of Arizona Press.

Fan, Maureen. 2008. "'Kung Fu Panda' Hits a Sore Spot in China, *Washington Post*, July 13, p. C-1f.

Finger, Charles J. 1924. *Tales from Silver Lands*. New York: Apple Paperbacks, Scholastic, copyright by Doubleday & Company.

Fink, Sam. 1994. "Reinventing Lincoln," *New Yorker*, November 14, p. 105.

Flesch, Rudolf. 1955. *Why Johnny Can't Read*. New York: Harper and Brothers.

Forbes, Esther. 1943. *Johnny Tremain*. New York: Houghton-Mifflin.

Frank, Anne. 1953. *The Diary of a Young Girl*. New York: Pocket Books.

Friesen, Helen. 1987. "Puzzle: Musically Speaking." *Modern Maturity Magazine*, August–September, p. 84.

Gardner, Howard. 1983. *Frames of Mind: The Theory of Multiple Intelligences.* New York: Basic Books.

Garner, James Finn. 1994. *Politically Correct Bedtime Stories.* New York: Macmillan.

Gedge, Pauline. 1977. *Child of the Morning.* New York: Soho Press.

George, Jean Craighead. 1972. *Julie of the Wolves.* New York: Harper Classics.

———. 1959. *My Side of the Mountain.* New York: Scholastic.

Gibbons, James Sloan, and Luther Orlando Emerson. 1862. "We Are Coming, Father Abraham." Civil War song available at www.pdmusic.org/civilwar.html.

Glazer, Steven A. 2007. "Where 'No Child' Fails." Letters to the Editor. *Washington Post*, September 15.

Grand Canyon National Park (video). 1988. Las Vegas: Norman Beeger Productions, VHS #18326.

Grimm's Fairy Tales. 1972. New York: Random House.

Hertzberg, Hendrik. 2007. "Talk of the Town: Comment." *New Yorker*, December 3, pp. 35–38.

Hesse, Karen. 1992. *Letters from Rifka.* New York: Scholastic.

———. 1997. *Out of the Dust.* New York: Scholastic.

Heyerdahl, Thor. 1990. *Kon Tiki.* New York: Simon and Schuster.

Hirsch, E. D., Jr. 1987. *Cultural Literacy: What Every American Needs to Know.* Boston: Houghton-Mifflin.

Hobbs, Will. 1992. *Downriver.* New York: Bantam Books.

Holbrook, Stewart H. 1953. *The Age of the Moguls: The Story of the Robber Barons and the Great Tycoons.* New York: Doubleday.

Holland, Barbara. 1990. "Vespucci Could Have Been Wrong, Right?" *Smithsonian*, March, p. 164.

Holmes, Joseph. 1996. *Grand Canyons of the Colorado.* San Francisco: Chronicle Books.

Hunt, Irene. 1993. *No Promises in the Wind.* New York: Berkley Books.

Jacobs, A. J. 1997. *Fractured Fairy Tales.* New York: Bantam Books.

Jensen, Eric. 1995. *Super Teaching.* San Diego: The Brain Store.

Juster, Norton. 1961. *The Phantom Tollbooth.* New York: Random House.

Ketcham, Hank. 2008. "Dennis, the Menace." *Washington Post*, November 2, Comic section.

Keys-Mathews, Lisa. 1998. *The Five Themes of Geography.* www2.una.edu/geography/statedepted/themes.html (last updated 1998).

REFERENCES

Kinsley, Michael. 1990. "Essay: These Foolish Things Remind Me of Diet Coke." *Time*, June 11, p. 88.

Kluger, Jeffrey. 2008. "The Art of Simplexity." *Time*, June 23, pp. 60–61.

Kyd, Thomas. 1987. *The Spanish Tragedy*. J. R. Mulryne, ed. New York: W. W. Norton.

Lasker, Joe. 1978. *Merry Ever After: The Story of Two Medieval Weddings*. New York: Penguin Books.

Laster, Madlon T. 2008. *Brain-based Teaching for All Subjects: Patterns to Promote Learning*. Lanham, MD: Rowman and Littlefield Education.

Leech, Margaret. 1962/1941. *Reveille in Washington 1860–1865*. New York: Time Inc.

Lehrer, Jim. 2008. *The NewsHour*, PBS-TV, WETA, Washington, DC, May 28.

Lieberman, Elias. 1965. "I Am an American." In *Poems that Live Forever*. New York: Doubleday.

Letters to the Editor. 2007. "Let Teachers Use Their Minds." *Washington Post*, July 7.

Levitin, Sonia. 1970. *Journey to America*. New York: Scholastic.

Lipson, M., S. Valencia, K. Wixson, and C. Peters. 1993. "Integration and Thematic Teaching: Integration to Improve Teaching and Learning." ERIC Document: Language Arts 70 (4), pp. 252–63 [EJ461 016].

London, Jack. 1982. "To Build a Fire." In *Literature and Life*, Medallion Series. Glenview, IL: Scott, Foresman, and Company.

Macaulay, David. 1977. *Castle*. New York: Houghton-Mifflin.

———. 1981. *Cathedral*. New York: Houghton-Mifflin.

Manigault, Charles. 1989. "This Scene of Destruction and Dismay, A Carolina Memoir: The Hurricane of 1822." *Washington Post*, October 1.

Masters, Edgar Lee. 1962. *Spoon River Anthology*. New York: Collier Books of Macmillan Publishing Company.

Mathews, Jay. 2008. "The Wrong Yardstick." *Washington Post Magazine*, April 13, p. 29ff.

McCain, M. N., and J. F. Mustard. 2007. "Early Years Study: Reversing the Real Brain Drain." In *Early Child Development from Measurement to Action*, Mary E. Young with Linda M. Richardson. Washington, DC: The World Bank.

Mears, Helen. 1953. *The First Book of Japan*. New York: Franklin Watts.

Meigs, Mildred Plew. 1952. "Abraham Lincoln." In *Time for Poetry: The Arbuthnot Anthology of Children's Literature*, Book 1. New York: Scott, Foresman and Company.

Meisel, Janet, et al. 1984. *Newscast from the Past*. PBS Series, with the University of Texas.

Miller, Allan. 1997. *Mad Amadeus Sued a Madam*. Boston: David R. Godine.

Miller, Joaquin. 1952. "Columbus." In *Time for Poetry: Anthology of Children's Literature*, Book 2. New York: Scott, Foresman and Company.

Minton, Lynn. 1990. "Fresh Voices." *Parade Magazine*, May 20.

Moberg, Vilhelm. 1949/1951. *The Emigrant Novels: Book 1—The Emigrants*. St. Paul: Minnesota Historical Society Press, 1949; translated 1951, additional material 1995.

Molfese, Dennis. 2007. "Reading and the Brain" (episode 8). *Launching Young Readers*: PBS-TV series.

Morrow, Lance. 1989. "When the Earth Cracks Open." *Time*, October 30, p. 100.

Mortenson, Greg, and David Oliver Relin. 2007. *Three Cups of Tea*. New York: Viking-Penguin.

"The Most Important Job." 2007. *New York Teacher*. www.nysut.org/cps/rde/xchg/nysut/hs.xsl/newyorkteacher_4183.htm, April 26, pp. 14–15.

"The Most Obedient Wife." 1952. In *Time for Fairy Tales: The Arbuthnot Anthology of Children's Literature*, Book 2. New York: Scott, Foresman and Company.

Moyers, Bill. 1984. *The Democrat and the Dictator* (film). PBS.

Murphy, Jim. 1993. *Across America on an Emigrant Train*. New York: Scholastic.

Naidu, Sarojini. 1969. "In the Bazaars of Hyderabad." In *A Book of Poetry*, J. Enright and Clara Marthaler, eds. New York: Harcourt, Brace, Javanovich.

Nash, Ogden. 1933. "Look What You Did, Christopher!" In *Happy Days*. New York: Simon and Schuster.

Nixon, Joan Lowery. 1994. *Land of Dreams*. Ellis Island Series. New York: Bantam Doubleday.

Norman, Donald. 1982. *Learning and Memory*. New York: Freeman and Co.

O'Dell, Scott. 1960. *Island of the Blue Dolphins*. New York: Dell Publishing Group.

Orwell, George. 1946. *Animal Farm*. New York: Harcourt Brace Jovanovich.

Paterson, Katherine. 1988. *Park's Quest*. New York: Viking-Penguin Puffin Books.

———. 1990. *The Tale of the Mandarin Ducks*. New York: Dutton.

Paulsen, Gary. 1987. *Hatchet*. New York: The Trumpet Club of Viking-Penguin.

Price, Willard. 1993. *African Adventure*. London: Random House, Red Fox edition.

Popescu, Roxana. "No Child Outside the Classroom." *Newsweek*, February 11, 2008, p. 12.

Ritter, Naomi. 1999. *Teaching Interdisciplinary Thematic Units in Language Arts*. ERIC Clearinghouse, Digest #142: EDO-CS-99-03, November.

Rittle-Johnson, Bethany. 2008. Quoted in "Kids Learn More When Mom Is Listening," *Ideas in Action*. Vanderbilt University-Peabody College. Nashville: University Press.

Robbins, Lisa. 2007. "Equity vs. Excellence." *Peabody Reflector*, Fall, pp. 17–21.

Robinson, Malcolm. 1988. *The American Vision: Landscape Paintings of the United States*. New York: Portland House.

Roets, Lois. 1986. *Leadership: A Skills Training Program, Ages 8–18*. Des Moines, IA: Leadership Press.

Rosenfeld, Megan. 1994. "And Now a Word about Sponsors . . ." *Washington Post*, May 8, p. G3.

Sagan, Carl. 1998. *Billions and Billions: Thoughts of Life and Death at the Brink of the Millennium*. New York: Random House.

Schambier, Robert F. 2007. "NCLB and Accountability." *Peabody Reflector*, Fall, p. 3.

Schlitz, Laura Amy. 2007. *Good Masters! Sweet Ladies! Voices from a Medieval Village*. Cambridge, MA: Candlewick Press.

Sciegaj, Catherine. 2008. "Five Themes in Geography." E-mail message to author, October 10.

Scieszka, Jon. 1991. *The Frog Prince Continued*. New York: Viking-Penguin.

———. 1989. *The True Story of the 3 Little Pigs!* New York: Scholastic Inc.

Silberger, Julius. 1952. "A Reply to Nancy Hanks." In *Time for Poetry: The Arbuthnot Anthology of Children's Literature*, Book 1. New York: Scott, Foresman and Company.

Sinclair, Upton. 1906/1985. *The Jungle*. New York: Penguin Classics.

Skurzynski, Gloria. 1992. *Lost in the Devil's Desert*. New York: Willowwisp Press of William Morrow.

Sperry, Armstrong. 1940/1963. *Call It Courage*. New York: Scholastic.

Sprenger, M. 1999. *Learning and Memory: The Brain in Action*. Alexandria, VA: ACDA.

Steinbeck, John. 1939. *The Grapes of Wrath*. New York: Viking Press; A Daryl Zanuck film, directed by John Ford, 1940.

Sweet 15: Facing Deportation. 1990. A WonderWorks Family Movie: Family Values Videos, #BWE0047.

Szoka, Roberta. 2008. E-mail message to author, June 7.

———. 2008. "What I've Learned about Thematic Teaching." E-mail message to author, August 5.

"Teacher of the Year: Marguerite Izzo." 2008. Segment on *The NewsHour with Jim Lehrer*, PBS-TV, WVPT, Harrisonburg, VA, September 28.

Thompson, Stith. 1966. *Tales of the North American Indians*. Bloomington: Indiana University Press.

Tomlinson, Carol. 1990. "Goldilocks and the Parts of Speech." Personal files. Faculty, Curry School of Education, University of Virginia, Charlottesville, VA.

Townsend, John Rowe. 1978. *Noah's Castle*. New York: Dell-Yearling of Random House.

Treffinger, D., and P. McEwen, 1989. *Fostering Independent Creative Learning*. Buffalo, NY: DOK Publishers.

Turner, Nancy Bird. 1952. "Lincoln." In *Time for Poetry: The Arbuthnot Anthology of Children's Literature*, Book 1. New York: Scott, Foresman and Company.

Uchida, Yoshiko. 1982. "The Bracelet." In *Literature and Life*. Glenview, IL: Scott, Foresman and Company.

Ullman, James Ramsey. 1954. *Banner in the Sky*. New York: Scholastic.

———. 1982. "Top Man." In *Literature and Life*, Medallion Series. Glenview, IL: Scott, Foresman and Company.

Utamaro, Kitigawa. n.d. "House Cleaning at the End of the Year" (woodcut). In *History of Art: A Survey of the Major Visual Arts from the Dawn of History to the Present Day*, H. W. Janson. New York: Harry N. Abrams.

Vygotsky, Lev. 1962. *Thought and Language*. Trans. E. Hanfmann and G. Vakar. Cambridge, MA: MIT Press.

Wallis, Claudia, and Sonja Steptoe. 2007. "How to Fix No Child Left Behind." *Time*, June 4, p. 34–41.

Warriner, John E., et al. 1978. *Grammar and Composition: First Course*. New York: Harcourt Brace Jovanovich.

Watson, W., and J. M. Nolte. 1955. *A Living Grammar*. St. Paul, MN: Itasca Press of Webb Publishing Company.

White, Robb. 1972. *Deathwatch*. New York: Laurel-Leaf of Dell Publishing Group.

Whitman, Walt. 1951. "O Captain! My Captain!" In *Best-Loved Poems*, Richard Charlton MacKenzie, ed. Garden City, NY: Permabooks.

———. 2001. "When Lilacs Last in the Dooryard Bloom'd." In *Concise Anthology of American Literature*, eds. George McMichael et al., fifth ed. Upper Saddle River, NJ: Prentice-Hall.

Whitney, Phyllis. 1958. *The Secret of the Samurai Sword*. Philadelphia: Westminster Press.

"Who is Shakespeare?" 1994. *Frontline Series*, PBS-TV, Boston: WGBH.

Willis, Aaron. Social Studies School Service, 10200 Jefferson Blvd. Culver City, CA, 90232.

Willis, Aaron, 2008. Interact of California at www.teachinteract.com. E-mail message to author, November 17.

REFERENCES

Wilder, Laura Ingalls. 1935. *Little House on the Prairie*. New York: Harper and Brothers.

Wills, Gary. 1992. "Dishonest Abe." *Time*, October 5, pp. 41–42.

Winn, Marie. 1978. *The Plug-in Drug*. New York: Bantam Books.

Winterfeld, Henry. 1956. *Detectives in Togas*. New York: Harcourt Brace Jovanovich.

Woodruff, Elvira. 1997. *The Orphan of Ellis Island*. New York: Scholastic.

Wrigley, Richard. 1992. *Ansel Adams: Images of the American West*. New York: Smithmark.

Wynne, Annette, 1952. "Columbus." In *Time for Poetry: The Arbuthnot Anthology of Children's Literature*, Book 1. New York: Scott, Foresman and Company.

Yashima, Taro. 1955. *Crow Boy*. New York: Viking Press.

Yep, Laurence. 1993. *Dragon's Gate*. New York: Scholastic.

———. 1982. "My True Name," from *Child of the Owl*. In *Purpose in Literature*. Glenview, IL: Scott, Foresman and Company.

———. 1982. "Paw-Paw," from *Child of the Owl*. In *Literature and Life*. Glenview, IL: Scott, Foresman and Company.

Young, Mary E. 2002. *From Early Child Development to Human Development*. Washington, DC: The World Bank.

Young, Mary E., with Linda M. Richardson. 2007. *Early Child Development: From Measurement to Action*. Washington, DC: The World Bank.

"Your Money: Making a Profit off Kids." 2007. *Parade Magazine*, October 28.

ABOUT THE AUTHOR

Madlon T. Laster completed her undergraduate work at Maryville College in Tennessee (1956). She taught in Wooster, Ohio, and at Community School in Tehran, Iran. While teaching in Tennessee, she earned her master's degree (1967) at George Peabody College for Teachers, now part of Vanderbilt University, Nashville. She and her husband lived in Beirut, Lebanon, from 1967 to 1973, during which time she taught methods courses, a children's literature course, and supervised student teachers at Beirut College for Women (BCW), now Lebanese American University. She completed her forty-two-year teaching career in Winchester City Schools, Winchester, Virgina, in the city's middle school, and earned her Ph.D. from George Mason University (1996). Her work for a certificate in cognitive instruction (1987) was earned through Radford University in Virginia.

Dr. Laster spent her career with the practical, or applied side, of instruction rather than publishing. She presented workshops in Zahleh, Lebanon, and traveled with Dr. Julinda AbuNasr of the BCW faculty to lead workshops on children's literature and libraries in Cairo, Egypt; Amman, Jordan; AbuDhabi, United Arab Emirates; and Bahrain. Following the workshops in December 1985 and January 1986, Drs. AbuNasr and Laster collaborated on a book about establishing children's libraries, which was published in Arabic. She has also made presentations with colleagues at various conferences and faculty workshops in Virginia.

This book is a companion volume to her first book, *Brain-based Teaching for All Subjects: Patterns to Promote Learning* (2008).

195